A Systematic Approach to Voice

The Art of Studio Application

A Systematic Approach to Voice

The Art of Studio Application

Kari Ragan

PLURAL
PUBLISHING
INC.

5521 Ruffin Road
San Diego, CA 92123

e-mail: information@pluralpublishing.com
Website: https://www.pluralpublishing.com

Typeset in 11/13 Garamond by Flanagan's Publishing Services, Inc.
Printed in the United States of America by Integrated Books International
24 23 22 21   4 5 6 7

Library of Congress Cataloging-in-Publication Data:
Names: Ragan, Kari, author.
Title: A systematic approach to voice : the art of studio application /
    Kari Ragan.
Description: San Diego, CA : Plural Publishing, Inc., [2020] | Includes
    bibliographical references and index.
Identifiers: LCCN 2020006683 | ISBN 9781635502237 (paperback) | ISBN
    1635502233 (paperback) | ISBN 9781635502305 (ebook)
Subjects: MESH: Voice Training | Voice Disorders—rehabilitation |
    Singing—physiology | Respiratory Physiological Phenomena
Classification: LCC RF540 | NLM WV 500 | DDC 616.85/56—dc23
LC record available at https://lccn.loc.gov/2020006683

Contents

Preface

I began teaching singing more than 35 years ago during my sophomore year of college. I am certain that I was far too young and inexperienced to be doing so and have often joked that those early students deserve a refund. My wonderful first college voice teacher at Pacific Lutheran University, Mrs. Barbara Poulshock, had faith that even as a young singer, I was capable of providing some insights to a group of students at a local high school. I could not have known the course that experience would set for my life. In the hubris of youth, I was going to be a SINGER, not a teacher—of that I was certain! And yet, through college, as a young emerging professional opera singer, and still today, I continue to passionately and gratefully make a living by teaching singing.

It is the essence and totality of those years that has led me to dare to write this book, a daunting task indeed. Before undertaking such a journey, one must ask what can possibly be contributed to the existing abundance of knowledge on teaching singing? I offer only this, through years of study with renowned voice teachers; earning a BM, MM, and DMA in vocal performance from prestigious universities; countless hours in lessons, coachings, and practice rooms; professional singing experience; relentless pedagogical study; extensive teaching experience (on average, 36 contact hours a week) both at the university level (graduates and undergraduates) and in independent studios (classical and CCM genres; teenagers, professionals, and avocational); and working in affiliation with a medical voice team to rehabilitate singers with injuries and pathologies, I have acquired a great deal of education, experience, and insight that I hope is useful. There is an ongoing need within the voice teaching profession to disseminate voice science knowledge by providing a pedagogic framework within voice studio application.

Some of what inspired the approach of this book can be attributed to Scott McCoy's seminal work, *Your Voice: An Inside View.*

I first discovered his book at a National Association of Teachers of Singing (NATS) conference shortly after its publication. As an Indiana University trained singer (BM and MM), I had previously taken a pedagogy course using Dr. Ralph Appleman's book *The Science of Voice Pedagogy*. However, with eyes on a singing career, I was not yet passionate about voice science since I did not understand the correlation to its application. Over the years, I read other influential pedagogy books. *Your Voice: An Inside View* uniquely resonated with me due to its structure, organization, and layout. The book presents science-informed principles of acoustics (resonance), respiration, phonation, articulation, and registration in an organized and accessible fashion. Its structure provides fact-based information without personal interpretation, philosophy, or teaching methodology. The lack of fixed teaching ideology was empowering because it allowed me to augment years of practice-based experience with fact-based information. It was neither in conflict to my teaching approach, nor did it require me to mold it into another's methodology. Instead, it provided evidence for answers I had been seeking. This enabled me to expand my knowledge, intuition, and creativity as an experienced teacher.

A Systematic Approach to Voice: The Art of Studio Application presents an organizational template integrating science-informed principles of voice production and pedagogical application in the training of singing artists. Of its eight chapters, five focus on the systems of voice production: respiration, phonation, registration, articulation, and resonance. Each of these voice system chapters contains an overview of the mechanics of its designated system and key points for teachers: "teacher takeaways." The unique focus of the book is to provide strategies for studio application by means of vocal exercises framed within a systematic approach.

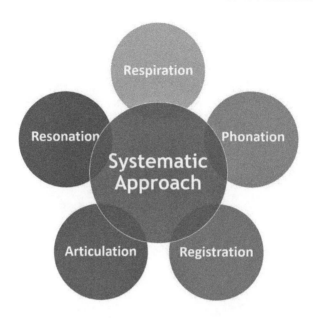

The history of voice pedagogy is compelling; it is a field fraught with misinformation and folklore. Yet, many historical pedagogues set a course for a singing technique that still holds, even if some of the semantics require translation through a fact-based approach. It is a privilege to carry on the legacy of great teaching artists. My ideas are the synthesis of so many extraordinary teachers, singing colleagues, voice scientists, laryngologists, speech-language pathologists, and authors to whom I am indebted. Most importantly, I am deeply grateful to each student who has collaborated with me on the journey to efficient and artistic singing!

Acknowledgments

I am immensely grateful to Joshua Langager who provided the musical notations and photos, in addition to calm, creative, and endless support along the way. A special thank you to students Darrell Jordan, Sarah Fantappie, Lauren Kulesa, Trevor Ainge, and Erika Meyer for their generosity of being picture models. Thank you, also, to the singers who graciously participated in the website companion video recordings of the exercises and sample warm-ups: Gemma Balinbin, Ryan Bede, Christopher Benefield, Robbie Christmas, Sarah Fantappie, Darrell Jordan, Lauren Kulesa, Josh Langager, Erika Meyer, Dawn Padula, Jordyn Palmer, Will Schlott, and Finley Skye.

I am deeply appreciative of my trusted colleagues whose contributions were invaluable and who were continuously available for expert advice and input: Kenneth Bozeman, BM; Mara Kapsner-Smith, MS, CCC-SLP; Michelle Bretl, BM, MS, CCC-SLP; and Dawn Padula, DMA. I wish to also thank Chadley Ballantyne, DMA, and Kerrie Obert, MA, CCC-SLP, whose contributions were instrumental to aspects of the resonance chapter (Chapter 7), and Abby Halpin, DPT, who provided crucial guidance to the respiration chapter (Chapter 3).

The synthesis of such an approach to teaching singing is influenced by teachers who generously gave of themselves throughout my life. Juilliard Emeritus Ellen Faull, with whom I trained for nearly 25 years, had a significant impact on both my singing and teaching careers. Miss Faull's influence is felt throughout the book. I am also grateful to the voice teachers from my early teens through college, including Dinah Lindberg Helgeson, Steve Harter, Barbara Poulshock, Martha Lipton, Lynn Luciano, Vinson Cole, and Barbara Robotham. I owe a debt of gratitude to my opera coach and friend, maestro Dean Williamson, who has been among my greatest teachers.

I wish to thank Yvette Litchfield (Chapters 1 and 2) and Daryl Ragan who contributed to editing portions of the book and were a constant source of encouragement. Further input was provided by the students in the Voice Pedagogy Application course at the University of Washington.

In the field of voice science and voice pedagogy, we stand on the shoulders of so many brilliant, generous colleagues across many disciplines. Many are found in the resources of each chapter. I am grateful for the contributions of those who have influenced our profession by providing a wealth of information, enabling an Evidence-Based Voice Pedagogy (EBVP) approach to teaching singing.

I greatly appreciate Plural Publishing for their support throughout this process, beginning with Brenda Smith who proposed me for this project; Valerie Johns, Executive Editor; Nicole Hodges, Assistant Editor; Christina Gunning, Project Editor; Lori Asbury, Production Manager; and Jessica Bristow, Production Assistant.

To my dear students, present and past, who continuously inspire me and without whom this book would not be possible— I truly have no words for the depth of my gratitude to each and every one of you. You honor me with the trust of the precious gift of your voice.

To my family and friends who have provided a lifetime of support through numerous professional pursuits, both performance and academic, I am deeply grateful. To my constant companion, Oliver, whose wags, cuddles, and insistence that I throw his rope toy and take time for daily walks in nature, brighten each day.

Reviewers

Plural Publishing, Inc. and the author would like to thank the following reviewers for taking the time to provide their valuable feedback during the development process:

Corbin Abernathy, BM, MPerfA, NATS, VASTA, EdTA, AEA
The Vocal Actor w/ Corbin Abernathy
Instructor of Voice
Penn State University, Abington Campus
Abington, Pennsylvania

Crystal Barron, MM, MDH
Breathing Coordination Advanced Practitioner
University of California, Irvine
Irvine, California

Patricia A. Boehm, BM, MM, PhD
Professor of Music
University of Mount Union
Alliance, Ohio

Karen Brunssen, BM
Associate Professor of Voice
Co-Chair of Music Performance
Bienen School of Music
Northwestern University
Evanston, Illinois
NATS President, 2018–2020

Robert Edwin, BA
Associate Editor
NATS Journal of Singing

Sarah Farr, DMA
Wayne State College
Wayne, Nebraska

Freda Herseth, DMHon, MM, BM
Arthur F. Thurnau Professor of Voice
School of Music, Theatre & Dance
Voice Training Specialist
Vocal Health Center
Department of Otolaryngology
University of Michigan
Ann Arbor, Michigan

Robert Peavler, DM, MM, BME
Professor of Voice
Eastern Michigan University
Ypsilanti, Michigan

Zipporah Peddle, MM, BM
Missouri State University
Springfield, Missouri

Ryan Townsend, MM, BFA
Instructor of Musical Theatre
Dobbins Conservatory of Theatre and Dance
Southeast Missouri State University
Cape Girardeau, Missouri

This book is dedicated to the many inspiring, fearless, remarkable singers with whom I have had the privilege of collaborating on a journey to efficient and artistic singing.

Chapter 1

A Systematic Approach

Although the art of singing can be learned only through singing, the systematic organization of vocal technique is the most efficient route to the realization of the primary goal: production of beautiful sound.

—Richard Miller, *The Structure of Singing* (1986), p. xxii

Introduction

This book does not advocate a particular *method* of teaching singing. It presents a systematic approach based on scientific principles that—together with a voice teacher's trained ears, intuition, creativity, and experience—guides singers toward technical proficiency. It is predicated on a belief that a systematic approach to teaching promotes efficient singing, which in turn enables great artistry. This book is born of decades of professional training and performance, as well as pedagogical study and teaching experience.

Teachers of singing have access to a wealth of information about the principles of voice production. There remains a need for a pedagogical framework in the service of studio application. This book presents an organizational template integrating science-informed principles of voice production and pedagogical application in the training of singing artists. Of its eight chapters, five focus on the systems of voice production: respiration, phonation, registration, articulation, and resonance. Each of the voice system chapters contains an overview of the mechanics of its designated system as well as key points for the teacher: "teacher takeaways."

1

A unique focus of the book is to provide strategies for studio application through vocal exercises framed within a systematic approach.

Voice science has provided the basis of this organizational template from which to teach singing in the form of the five voice systems. Knowledge of both the *independence* and *interdependence* of these systems enables teachers to devise strategies for the training of a functional singing technique. The use of *science-informed imagery* can further elicit a kinesthetic response and promote understanding for singers. There are many layers to structuring a successful voice lesson. While artistry is an essential component of performance, a primary responsibility of the voice teacher is to guide the development of a reliable singing technique. Structuring voice lessons through a science-informed foundation enables teachers to build a dependable, systematic approach, and also provides an effective way to identify technical challenges, design corrective exercises, and create strategies for developing vocal efficiency.

Voice teachers are much like Sherlock Holmes: they investigate technical challenges based on keen aural and visual observation. Rather than conjecture, a systematic approach provides a fact-based framework within which technical inefficiencies may be identified. It enables teachers to select, design, and sequence vocal exercises through a systematic lens based on principles of voice mechanics, remembering, of course, that changing one part of the system affects other parts and the whole. Employing a systematic approach based on a science-informed foundation provides the teacher with the full range of possible pathways to guide singers toward solutions. When the process is organized in this fashion, the teacher and student benefit because there is less speculation. The art of teaching is knowing how to facilitate and elicit the desired vocal outcome.

While the teacher provides guidance and direction during a lesson, singing habilitation occurs with daily practice away from the teacher. A systematic approach enables the student to more accurately replicate the successful aspects of the lesson experience during individual practice sessions because goals and strategies are more clearly established. Teachers do not teach someone how to sing so much as *how to practice*. A teacher provides the knowledge and structure to facilitate vocal efficiency so that a student gains a comprehensive understanding of optimal practice habits for long-term skill acquisition. These improved practice habits result in more immediate results that ultimately lead to a consistent and reliable singing technique.

A teacher's knowledge, intuition, and creativity are essential to the art of studio application. Vennard wrote, "A versatile teacher tries as many approaches as possible until he discovers the one that works for each pupil" (Vennard, 1968 p. 191). A systematic approach enables a collaborative exploration of a singer's technique with the individual needs of the student in mind. This approach empowers teachers to adapt to the genre and skill level of a singer because the principles of voice production provide a foundation from which to build. Constructive voice lessons help the singer engage in the learning *process* actively, not merely focus on achieving an *outcome*. When teachers acquire fact-based knowledge of the voice systems as their foundational approach, even as voice science evolves, a strategy for training a functional singing technique remains dependable as the baseline.

A Systematic Approach

- Provides a template of systematic organization of respiration, phonation, registration, articulation, and resonance
- Enables more effective identification of technical vocal challenges
- Allows the design of vocal exercises based on knowledge of the *independence* and *interdependence* of the voice systems
- Creates an understanding for sequencing corrective vocal exercises for developing technical efficiency
- Generates reliable and consistent results for singers
- Enables efficient singing to be achieved more quickly
- Is applicable to any genre and any skill level because the fundamentals of efficient singing provide a dependable foundation
- Allows for refinement within a systematic approach as singing voice science evolves

The Heuristic Nature of a Systematic Approach

A heuristic teaching method is one that encourages students toward experimentation and guided discovery. It empowers students to explore through an individual learning style. A systematic approach provides a template for clearly understanding the principles of voice production, and thereby stimulates the self-inquiry necessary to support a heuristic teaching method. This leads the student to better self-efficacy and autonomy. A heuristic teaching method inspires students to become lifelong learners and encourages independent investigation because they feel empowered by a foundation of knowledge. This enables singers to seek answers through trial, error, and experimentation. They learn to trust their instincts. A singer's ability to evaluate their practice is invaluable in facilitating technical progress and, in time, prowess.

There is a tradition in the field of voice teaching whereby a student finishes a song and immediately looks to the teacher to evaluate the success or failure of their singing, either by facial expression, gesture, or commentary. This is a necessary process at various stages of skill acquisition. However, students can become too dependent on the teacher's response, preventing long-term gains (Verdolini, 1997). A heuristic method empowers the student by making the lessons student-centric rather than teacher-centric. It does not diminish the importance of mentorship and guidance; instead, it encourages a collaborative dynamic between the teacher (advanced learner) and student (learner). It fosters mutual respect by honoring the student's process as an integral part of the learning experience. Singers are empowered to engage in the learning process, working toward autonomy in their journey to efficient and artistic singing.

Kinesthetic Singing Tools

Kinesthetic singing tools are introduced throughout the book. These tools are used to elicit a positive kinesthetic response—a perceptual, physical, or acoustical adjustment during singing habilitation. Since singers spend the majority of their practice time away from the guidance of the teacher, these tools support reliable practice sessions. By providing structure, kinesthetic singing tools lead to improved accuracy in developing new motor skills. These tools can provide a more expeditious approach to a new and replicable sensory experience than ongoing explanations by a teacher. Voice teachers can be easily trapped in verbal explanations during the singing lesson. However, research has found that such verbal explanations have limited efficacy as a teaching or learning device (Verdolini, 1997). As with any vocal function exercise, the teacher and student must recognize the intent and understand the application of the kinesthetic singing tool in order to achieve the benefits.

Kinesthetic singing tools are presented within each systematic chapter for which they are tailored. Chapter 3, the respiration chapter, presents a barre3 ball, a large exercise ball, a Futuro Surgical Abdominal Support, a Flow-ball by POWERbreathe, and an exercise band as kinesthetic singing tools to develop effective breath mechanics. Chapter 4, the phonation chapter, describes the benefits of using semi-occluded vocal tract exercises, such as straws and water bubbles, for developing vocal efficiency. Chapter 6, the articulation chapter, introduces gauze, candy, and wine corks as useful tools for deconstructing patterns of recruitment. Chapter 7, the resonance chapter, presents the use of a chopstick, the singer's thumb, and a mirror. Kinesthetic singing tools are beneficial to the process of habilitation and for the correction of a variety of vocal challenges. They aid in eiliminating extraneous muscle activity, which must precede the work of training new singing strategies. Throughout the process, new patterns of coordinated voice production develop. The goal is to use the kinesthetic singing tools until such a time as they are no longer needed. Once long-term skill acquisition is achieved, the tools need only be used as an infrequent reset.

It is perplexing that kinesthetic singing tools are sometimes dismissed as tricks. Unlike other athletes who depend on visible outcomes, singers must rely upon internalized physical sensations, rendering kinesthetic singing tools both necessary and particularly useful. Baseball players, football players, and golfers have the benefit of seeing results by the trajectory of a ball, whereas singers learn without a visible representation of their efforts. Kinesthetic singing tools are a valid addition to a practice regimen because they provide both visible and sensory feedback during the learning process.

Alterations of Vocal Exercises

A teacher's intuition and knowledge guide the direction of a voice lesson and determine how to adapt and modify the vocal exercises presented in this book. Alterations are anticipated in order to accommodate the individual needs of the singer, including technical considerations or stylistic diversity. These modifications will depend on the voice type and skill level of a singer and on genre-informed strategies. Some alterations to be considered are range, rhythmic patterns (e.g., syncopation), harmonic structure (e.g., major to minor), tempo, vibrato choices (e.g., whether to delay the vibrato or allow at vocal onset), and a continuum of resonance strategies determined by stylistic elements of a particular genre. The vocal exercises are presented within a systematic approach to a functional singing technique, enabling excursions into a broad range of vocal aesthetics across genres. Although emotive cues are not included within the exercises, singers will find it helpful to use the association of an emotion as a reminder that the ultimate goal of performing is to communicate thoughts and feelings. At some point in vocal training, artistry and technique must be juxtaposed. The art of teaching entails successful collaboration between teacher and student in assessing and modifying the exercises to facilitate optimal outcomes.

It is *not* the job of the voice teacher to diagnose beyond the scope of technical inefficiency. If a student presents with an ongoing vocal health concern, they must be referred to a qualified laryngologist or otolaryngologist-voice specialist and potentially to a voice team (Ragan, 2017). A voice teacher may be inclined to conjecture a medical diagnosis but must adhere to their scope of practice and refer to voice team specialists when necessary.

Summary

This book presents a framework for the integration of science-informed principles of voice production and pedagogical application in the training of singers. This framework acknowledges the importance of genre-specific and stylistic elements that, when layered on the foundation of a functional singing technique, enables artistic integrity. Learning to sing is a lifelong journey. There is no point of arrival for the singing artist, rather an ever-evolving destination. Singers must be encouraged to embrace the process and "buckle up and enjoy the ride." Even when proficiency in singing technique is attained, there will be constant recalibration within the voice systems as each new song brings subtle alterations to the many facets of technique and artistry. Ongoing physiological changes will continue to impact the voice across the span of a lifetime. The joy in the journey is that with each passing year, a singer has richer life experience from which to draw for artistic expression.

References

Miller, Richard. (1986). *The Structure of Singing*. Belmont, CA: Schirmer.

Ragan, K. (2017). Understanding voice doctors: Who to call and when to call them. *Journal of Singing, 74*(1), 57–62.

Vennard, W. (1968). *Singing: The mechanics and the technic* (5th ed.). New York, NY: Carl Fischer.

Verdolini, K. (1997). Principles of skill acquisition applied to voice training. In M. Hampton & B. Acker (Eds.), *The vocal vision: Views on voice by 24 leading teachers, coaches and directors* (pp. 65–81). New York, NY: Applause.

Selected Resource

Brunssen, K. (2018). *The evolving singing voice: Changes across the lifespan*. San Diego, CA: Plural Publishing.

Chapter 2

The Twenty-First Century Voice Teacher

Technique is inseparable from art. Only by mastering the technique of his material is the artist in a condition to mould his mental work of art and to again give it—his possession borrowed from life—to others. Even artists intellectually highly gifted remain crippled without this mastery of the technique.

—Lilli Lehmann, *How to Sing* (1914), p. vi

Introduction

Voice pedagogy encompasses the art and science of teaching singing. It is the study of anatomy, physiology, acoustics, and cognition in the training of singers, as well as the application of those principles in the service of an artistic outcome. Sound knowledge of these pillars as well as familiarity with the systems of voice production as they apply to the musical genre(s) in which their students sing should be the core of any singing teacher's pedagogy. While voice science makes a significant contribution to understanding the mechanics of singing, it is still incumbent upon the teacher to know how to disseminate the information within the structure of a lesson. Voice teachers must be skilled at translating a science-informed approach in the context of studio application.

In 2014, the American Academy of Teachers of Singing (AATS) published a paper entitled "In Support of Fact-Based Voice

Pedagogy and Terminology." It states, "Voice science does not tell us what to do as teachers of singing: it tells us what is happening during the act of singing. Science informs art, it does not create it." (AATS, 2014) Teaching singing requires utilizing science-informed strategies in pursuit of an artistic endeavor. The quest for voice teachers is to become proficient at building a bridge between art and science in training the performing artist. Victor Fields writes:

> . . . singing is both science and art. Science is concerned largely with laws, rules and techniques, with methodology, purposes and goals; while art is concerned with finished outcomes, with the perfected expression. Science may be regarded as the *means;* art the *end* of learning. (Fields, 1972, p. 22)

The art of studio application is found on a continuum between art and science, athlete and artist.

Singing is a field in which efforts are ultimately in service of the physical demands of *doing.* Voice teachers must find a clear way to impart science-based information without excessive discourse that traps either the teacher or singer in *thinking* to the extent that they are *intellectualizing* rather than performing. Each singer mentally interprets and kinesthetically experiences the information in their own way—the journey toward technical and artistic mastery is a process as unique as the individual singer. Voice teaching must be personalized and flexible, while grounded in the principles of voice production that equip teachers with the science necessary to facilitate the artistic expression they are guiding.

Decades of research have contributed to a paradigm shift within the field of voice teaching from an approach that was historically imagery-based to one balanced with the inclusion of science-based knowledge. It is increasingly evident that knowledge of the principles of voice production benefits teachers and the singers in their care. This cultural shift has moved the profession toward a more nuanced understanding of the five systems of voice production, including greater specificity concerning aspects of genre. An approach to singing based on voice function *discourages* values being placed on one genre over another and *encourages* effective teaching practices. The voice, in this way, is considered an instrument to be trained without boundaries or limitations imposed by musical genre. Style-specific elements generally evolve after efficient singing is achieved, though at some points, they may develop in tandem (this does not negate the extensive pedagogical differences in training various genres).

Cross-Training the Voice Athlete

Singers are now recognized as voice athletes. Cross-training principles founded in exercise science should be integrated into professional voice training. Translating and applying this science to voice training, however, should be undertaken with some caution (Sandage & Pascoe, 2010). In cross-training, the voice athlete must condition their instrument through a wide variety of exercises to achieve healthy and efficient singing. The authors of *The Vocal Athlete* state,

> As with all physical actions, voice production requires a combination of muscular strength and coordination of multiple body systems even for the most basic phonatory tasks. Consider the complex mental, physical, and vocal actions necessary for high-level singing, regardless of style. Although there are physiological differences in how these styles are produced, all genres of singing require stable, strong musculature functioning in a balanced, efficient manner for optimal output. (LeBorgne & Rosenberg, 2015, p. 243)

Training a balanced mechanism across genres is a fundamental principle of cross-training for beneficial application in the voice studio. This approach improves overall vocal function and renders the singer more versatile and employable.

There is a growing trend in the classical music industry for opera and musical theatre to live under the same roof (McQuade, McQuade, Henderson, & Sisco, 2018). This departure from the tradition of genres living independently has become necessary due to cultural and fiscal changes. Voice training programs must evolve to accommodate the needs of singing artists as they prepare for this cross-genre industry transition. The authors of the recent book *Cross-Training in the Voice Studio* write,

> What seems to be happening is, in fact, a cultural shift, a gradual artistic union of these two art forms in a way that enriches both while maintaining the valuable distinctions between them. It is becoming

difficult for classical voice teachers to insulate themselves from this new reality. (Spivey & Barton, 2018, p. 23)

The music industry is changing, and so must a voice teacher's pedagogical approach in order to meet the needs of the 21st century singer.

Academic voice teachers are often hired to teach within a specific genre and curriculum. As cross-training principles increasingly contribute to a functional singing technique and sustainable singing career, academic teachers will find it beneficial to have pedagogical knowledge of voice production and stylistic approaches as they apply to various genres. There is a current trend in academic job postings to request that candidates have pedagogical knowledge in multiple styles, both classical and contemporary commercial music (CCM). Independent teachers, whose studios now comprise singers of various genres, also require this same breadth of pedagogical knowledge. This is a significant shift from the tradition of teaching voice predominantly in one genre.

Independent voice studios are thriving in the 21st century; maintaining a business teaching singing is more feasible than ever. Consequently, many highly educated, skilled voice teachers are choosing not to enter into the academic environment. Modern technology, particularly the Internet and the inception of social media, has broadened the possibilities even further with the introduction of online lessons, career-forging television shows, and Internet-based marketing. From a business perspective, specializing in a specific genre would disadvantage the majority of independent studio teachers. There are those exceptions who have successfully built studios focused on only one genre—often following a distinguished career within that genre. However, the vast majority of independent studio teachers will need a comprehensive pedagogy in a broad range of genres to maintain a thriving business.

Voice Habilitation

There are no magic vocal exercises! There are exercises designed to facilitate a particular change in vocal function. The potential for a given exercise to work is contingent on the intention of the exercise, the instruction provided, and the singer's understanding and implementation. Ideally, a teacher will select, through a pedagogical lens of the appropriate voice system, vocal exercises supported by either quantifiable research or validated by anecdotal practice-based evidence. Vocal exercises are designed to train the voice by developing endurance, strength, and coordination. This process is called voice habilitation and is defined as *"enabling, equipping for,* or *capacitating"* the voice to meet very specific demands (Titze & Verdolini Abbott, 2012, p. 11). There are no magic vocal exercises found within this process but informed strategies that expertly guide the training of singers toward a dependable singing technique.

It is the responsibility of voice teachers to identify vocal inefficiencies and provide corrective strategies to develop practice habits for long-term skill acquisition. James McKinney identifies three basic questions voice teachers must ask themselves:

1. What is wrong with the sound I am hearing?
2. What is causing it to sound that way?
3. What am I going to do about it?

He states that voice teachers must *recognize symptoms, determine causes,* and *devise cures,* much like a medical doctor (McKinney, 1994, p. 17). The process of identifying a technical challenge and designing and sequencing a corrective task is an integral part of a voice teacher's responsibilities. The good news is that "many roads lead to Rome." Implementing a systematic approach based on a functional understanding of the five voice systems provides the teacher with the full range of possible pathways to guide singers toward solutions. For example, a vocal function exercise focused on resonance will, at times, be more effective than one focused on respiration, yet an approach via either system of voice production may yield a positive outcome. A singer's individual needs, learning style, and feedback are integral in guiding the process of deciding on which voice system to focus a given exercise.

A Vocal Warm-Up Versus Vocal Function Exercises

There is a significant distinction of *intent* between vocal function exercises and vocal warm-ups. (This is *not* in reference to Stemple's vocal function exercises (VFE's) used in voice therapy.) Vocal function exercises and vocal warm-ups may appear to be the same since both, constructed of musical patterns, are used to facilitate the act of singing. Although quantitative research is ongoing to explain with greater specificity their benefits, anecdotal evidence certainly supports their efficacy. There is an important difference, however, in that a vocal warm-up occurs before a practice session, lesson, coaching, audition, or performance. A vocal warm-up is designed specifically to *prepare* the instrument for the demands of the intended task, where vocal function exercises are targeted to enable the singer to *do* the intended task. Unlike vocal function exercises, a vocal warm-up focuses solely on the present moment and might be achieved in a matter of minutes, depending on the singer's individual needs and circumstances. Being focused on the present moment enables a vocal warm-up to serve the important psychological function of promoting a state of mindfulness in the singer. A vocal warm-up facilitates the necessary interaction of the physical and mental aspects of preparing to sing.

Vocal function exercises are often the same vocal tasks used in a warm-up but with an intention toward habilitation for long-term skill acquisition. Vocal function exercises are selected or designed as a specific corrective task to develop, coordinate, strengthen, improve, and balance the systems of the voice for singing. In order to acquire a permanent change in the technical ability to execute efficient singing, the approach to a vocal function exercise is significantly different to that of a vocal warm-up. A vocal function exercise is often designed spontaneously to train the specific technical needs of a singer in the moment. The procedure will be individual and the methodology flexible. The pacing of a vocal function exercise is distinct as the process may be interrupted to correct a vocal challenge, provide guidance, and then repeated several times to facilitate "muscle memory." A vocal exercise will instinctively increase or decrease in difficulty to accommodate the individual student. The choices during this process are student driven and teacher prescribed.

Motor Learning Theory and the Singer

The importance of cognitive science as it applies to voice pedagogy continues to advance. Lynn Helding has outlined a precedent that includes the human mind as the third pillar of voice pedagogy alongside physiology and voice acoustics (Helding, 2019, p. 280). This is an essential shift in the profession. Within the context of cognitive science are the inclusion of topics such as neuroplasticity, perception, procedural learning, and motor learning theory. The definition of motor learning used by Helding states, "motor learning is a **process**, which is **inferred** rather than directly observed, which leads to **permanent changes** in **habit** as the result of **experience** or **practice**" (Helding, 2019, p. 292). You may recall your voice teacher saying, "now you have got it . . . go practice it a thousand times!" It turns out there was truth in that assertion. For voice teachers, knowledge of motor learning principles will guide the process of structuring a voice lesson and a singer's practice session for successful long-term skill acquisition. The scope of this book does not extend to the extensive and important subject of the application of cognitive science and motor learning theory in training singers. Readers seeking more detail on the subject are encouraged to review this chapter's selected resources.

Summary

Voice teachers have a tremendous responsibility to singers who rely on their expertise. The dynamic relationship between the voice teacher and the singer is complex and requires empathy, compassion, and intuition. The teacher holds a position of authority over a musical instrument that resides within the body and impacts closely on the identity and spirit of another human being. Voice teachers have a profound role in the lives of the singers who place significant trust in them. It is a privilege that must be pursued with the utmost integrity.

A recent paper published by this author presented a framework for defining what is termed Evidence-Based Voice Pedagogy (EBVP; Ragan, 2018). This new framework includes three essential components of voice teaching: voice research (including historical pedagogy), voice teacher expertise and experience (practice-based research), and student goals and perspectives (the individual's needs) (Figure 2–1).

Experienced voice teachers understand the value of juxtaposing fact-based and practice-based voice pedagogy within a lesson.

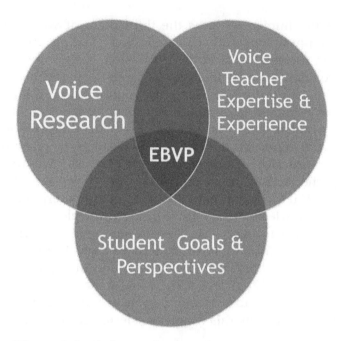

Figure 2–1. An image representing the three components of evidence-based voice pedagogy (EBVP).

In that environment, anecdotal evidence is an equal partner to scientific evidence. Pedagogical truths may come from a variety of sources to serve the complex needs of the individual trusting the teacher. This book is the synthesis of that approach.

References

The Academy of American Voice Teachers (AATS). (2014). *In support of fact-based voice pedagogy and terminology.* Retrieved from http://www.americanacademyofteachersofsinging.org/assets/articles/CCM VoicePedagogy.pdf

Elliot, N., Sundberg, J., & Gramming, P. (1995). What happens during vocal warm-up? *Journal of Voice, 9*(1), 37–44.

Fields, V. (1972). Art versus science in singing. *The NATS Bulletin*, pp. 22–29.

Helding, L. (2019). Brain. In S. McCoy, (Ed.), *Your voice: An inside view* (3rd ed., pp. 279–306). Delaware, OH: Inside View Press.

LeBorgne, W., & Rosenberg, M. (2015). *The vocal athlete*. San Diego, CA: Plural Publishing.

Lehmann, L. (1914). How to sing. New York, NY: MacMillan Company.

McKinney, J. (1994). *The diagnosis & correction of vocal faults*. Long Grove, IL: Waveland Press.

McQuade, M., McQuade, J., Henderson, A., & Sisco, D. (2018). Cinderella meets Cendrillon: Music theater and opera living under the same roof. *Journal of Singing, 75*(2), 121–130.

Ragan, K. (2018). Defining evidence-based voice pedagogy: A new framework. *Journal of Singing, 75*(2), 157–160.

Sandage, M. J., & Pascoe, D. (2010). Translating exercise science into voice care: Perspectives on voice and voice disorders. *American Speech and Language Hearing Association, 20*(3), 84–89.

Spivey, N., & Barton, M. S. (2018). *Cross-training in the voice studio: A balancing act*. San Diego, CA: Plural Publishing.

Titze, I., & Verdolini Abbott, K. (2012). *Vocology: The science and practice of voice habilitation*. Salt Lake City, UT: National Center for Voice and Speech.

Selected Resources

Bergan, C. (2010). Motor learning principles and voice pedagogy: Theory and practice. *Journal of Singing, 66*(4), 457–468.

Elliot, N., Sundberg, J., & Gramming, P. (1995). What happens during vocal warm-up? *Journal of Voice, 9*(1), 37–44.

Helding, L. (2007). Voice science and vocal art, part one: In search of common ground. *Journal of Singing, 64*(2), 141–150.

Helding, L. (2008). Voice science and vocal art, part two: Motor learning theory. *Journal of Singing, 64*(4), 417–428.

Helding, L. (2017). Cognitive dissonance: Facts versus alternative facts. *Journal of Singing, 74*(1), 89–93.

Helding, L. (2020). *The musician's mind: Teaching learning, and performance in the age of brain science*. Lanham, MD: Rowan and Littlefield.

Maxfield, L. (2013). Improve your students' learning by improving your feedback. *Journal of Singing, 69*(4), 471–478.

Nisbet, A. (2003). *Singing teachers talk too much*. Retrieved from http://hdl.handle.net/10072/1858

Nix, J. (2017). Best practices: Using exercise physiology and motor learning principles in the teaching studio and the practice room. *Journal of Singing, 74*(2), 215–220.

Sandage, M. J., & Hoch, M. (2018). Exercise physiology: Perspective for vocal training. *Journal of Singing,* 74(4), 419–425.

Schmidt, R., Lee, T., Winstein, C., Wulf, G., & Zelaznik, H. (2019). *Motor control and learning: A behavioral emphasis* (6th ed). Champagne, IL: Human Kinestics.

Titze, I., & Verdolini, K. (2012). Perceptual motor learning principles: How to train. In I. R. Titze & K. Verdolini (Eds.), *Vocology* (pp. 217–238). Iowa City, IA: National Center for Voice and Speech.

Williams, J. (2019). *Warm-ups for singers: What exactly are we trying to achieve?* Retrieved from http://www.jenevorawilliams.com/online-resources/

Chapter 3

A Systematic Approach to Respiration

Rigidity is the enemy of breathing, and indeed of any muscular endeavor. Unfortunately, all too often attempts to produce vocal power originate with rigid breathing habits. In the like manner, if singers struggle to conserve air by holding it in, they will not only induce an amazing amount of muscular tension, but actually will lose more air than if the attempt had never been made. Holding back air is rather like an athlete trying to run with the brakes on.

—Barbara Doscher, *Functional Unity of the Singing Voice*
(1994), p. 25

Overview of Respiration

The respiratory system is considered the power source of voice production. In singing, all the systems of the voice must be coordinated and in balance; however, the influence of breath management cannot be overestimated. In part, a singer's breath management requires a dynamic balance between inspiratory and expiratory muscles to achieve efficiency. Coordination of the muscles to regulate subglottal air pressure and airflow is essential to proper technique. When considering the system of respiration for singers, both inhalation and exhalation phases of breath management must be considered. One without the other is analogous to a tennis coach teaching a player the backhand but not the forehand. To be a successful tennis player, one must have a high level of skill at both phases of swinging a tennis racket. Similarly, singing requires two phases of respiratory skill acquisition: inhalation and exhalation.

Inhalation

The two primary muscles of inhalation are the diaphragm and external intercostals (Figure 3–I). Along with several secondary (accessory) inspiratory muscles, they form a complex network to contribute to a singer's breath management. By initiating the inhalation of air for singing, a process is set in motion that enables

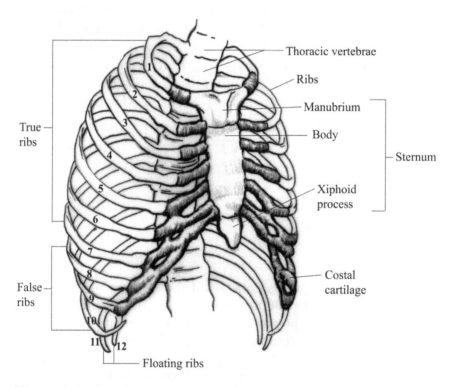

Figure 3–I. The rib cage (thorax). From *Voice Technique: A Physiologic Approach* (2nd ed., p. 17), by J. E. Bickel, 2017, San Diego, CA: Plural Publishing. Copyright 2018 by Plural Publishing. Used with permission.

the expansion of the rib cage (thorax) and abdominal cavities, creating a negative pressure within the lungs. Boyle's law—named for Robert Boyle, a 17th-century British scientist—explains that when a gas, such as air, is contained in an enclosure, pressure and volume are inversely related. When volume increases, it causes a proportional decrease in pressure; and, conversely, when pressure increases, it causes a proportional decrease in volume. During inhalation, active expansion of the rib cage and abdominal cavities generates *more* volume and *less* air pressure in the thorax and lungs. Since nature abhors a vacuum, atmospheric pressure then seeks to equalize the situation by moving air into the lungs.

For singers, the outward movement of the rib cage is due to muscle *contraction* (diaphragm and external intercostal muscles) and the presence of the internal organs beneath the rib cage resisting downward movement (passive gravitational resistance), while the outward abdominal wall movement is due to a *release* of the core muscles' contractions. Although both the rib cage and abdominal wall move in an outward direction, active control of the muscles must be distinguished between contraction or release. This is an important distinction for the singing practitioner. The rib cage is formed by 12 thoracic vertebrae, the sternum, and the costal cartilages (see Figure 3–1). The ability of the rib cage to expand upward and outward is due to flexible joints that allow for a significant range of lateral (side to side) and anteroposterior (front and back) motion. When the breathing process initiates, the dimensional change in the diameter of the rib cage, either larger or smaller, contributes to the act of breathing. Often, singers focus solely on the front of the body. However, during inhalation, posterior thoracic expansion in addition to anterior and lateral expansion is necessary. Singers must be mindful to not inadvertently hold unwanted tension in the back while releasing only the front of the abdominal wall.

The diaphragm is an important and often misunderstood muscle. It is a large dome-shaped muscle that separates the contents of the thoracic and abdominal cavities. When the diaphragm contracts, it contributes to increasing the size of the rib cage and lungs (aided by the pleural sac), creating the air pressure differential previously mentioned. The diaphragmatic contraction displaces the internal organs through its downward motion. For the diaphragmatic muscle to descend quickly, as is often needed in singing, abdominal muscles must release any held tension to allow some expansion of the abdominal wall for the displaced viscera (although there will still be some tonicity in the core muscles). Biologically, the diaphragm is exclusively a muscle of inspiration and generally passive during expiration as it returns to its natural (at rest) state before the breathing cycle repeats. During phonation, however, singers may use varying diaphragmatic contraction as an antagonist during exhalation to control breath pressure and airflow (McCoy, 2019, p. 124). It appears that the role of the diaphragm varies in different singers and that coactivation of the diaphragm and abdominal wall muscles during exhalation may be a part of a singer's breath management strategy (Sundberg, 1987, pp. 31–32).

It must be noted that singers do not have an explicit sensory perception of the diaphragm, which technically is a voluntary muscle but over which it is difficult to have direct control. Singers learn to perceive diaphragmatic activity by means of thoracic and abdominal movement. Unfortunately, the phrase "breathe from your diaphragm" (which all breathing involves) or "sing from your diaphragm" (which is not possible) are persistent misnomers among singing teachers.

Exhalation

The six primary muscles of exhalation are the internal intercostal, rectus abdominis, internal and external oblique, transverse abdominus, and quadratus lumborum (Figure 3–II). These muscles also function to stabilize and move the torso (trunk). Along with several secondary (accessory) expiratory muscles, they form a complex network to contribute to a singer's breath management. During active exhalation, muscles contract changing the intra-abdominal pressure by making the rib cage smaller and compressing the abdominal viscera. This, according to Boyle's law, creates a decrease in the volume and an increase in the pressure, which causes air to rush out of the lungs. There is also the important aspect of elastic recoil of the system that significantly contributes to the process of exhalation. Elastic recoil is a rebound of the lungs after having been stretched during inhalation. The muscles

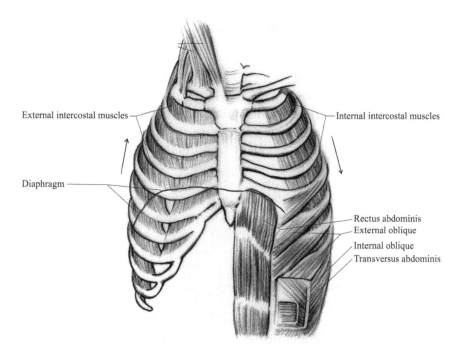

Figure 3–II. The primary muscles of inhalation and exhalation (with the exception of the quadratus lumborum [not pictured]). Modified from *Voice Technique: A Physiologic Approach* (2nd ed., p. 20), by J. E. Bickel, 2017, San Diego, CA: Plural Publishing. Copyright 2018 by Plural Publishing. Used with permission.

of inhalation provide a checking action at the height of the breath when recoil is strongest, then the management transitions to active use of expiratory muscles as lung volumes decrease and recoil is less. The nuanced control of this dynamic system requires training for singers. Because singers need to control the rate at which air expels from the lungs, there is an important antagonistic relationship between muscles of inhalation and exhalation. An example of the necessary respiratory antagonism for efficient singing is the dynamic relationship between the external intercostal muscles (primary inhalation) that elevate the ribs and the oblique abdominal muscles (primary exhalation) that depress the ribs. Due to points of attachment and insertion of these muscles, the antagonistic relationship contributes to a singer's breath management.

Teacher Takeaways of Respiration

As voice athletes, the dynamic nature of breathing for singing is at the core of efficient voicing. To teach this effectively, it is necessary to understand the fundamentals of respiratory mechanics. For example, by understanding Boyle's law of physics, one learns that they do not need to suck or gasp air during inhalation since it can result in an unnecessary audible inhalation and create unwanted tension in the respiration, phonation, or articulation systems. Instead, air enters the lungs when the expanding thoracic and abdominal cavities create more room in the body, as previously described.

The fundamentals of respiratory mechanics explain that during exhalation, antagonism is a necessary part of a singer's breath management strategy. Breath management refers to control of steady airflow being expelled from the lungs after taking a larger breath during inhalation necessary for singing. It takes a great deal of training for a singer to master this critical, coordinated effort. Teachers must guide an approach to learning breath management skills that enables the kinesthetic exploration of muscles to be active and engaged *but not rigid*.

Breath mechanics, at some point, must be discussed in relation to the critical and coordinated effort of the phonation system. There is a dynamic relationship that exists between these two systems since the vocal folds, housed within the larynx, participate in the regulation of airflow by providing a variable resistance to air being expelled from the lungs during phonation. The interdependency between these two systems is also important because the larynx converts aerodynamic energy into acoustic energy in voice production. Optimal posture and alignment provide stability of the larynx, which exemplifies this intricate relationship. There are extrinsic laryngeal muscles that attach to the sternum, which move and stabilize the larynx. With control, consistency, and stability in the mechanics of breathing for singing, the laryngeal position is anchored. This allows for independence of muscle activation between the respiration and phonation systems. This collaboration prevents overactivation of extrinsic laryngeal muscles that may compensate for unwanted activation of secondary respiratory muscles. In essence, respiratory stability, in conjunction with laryngeal stability, prevents unwanted compensatory engagement of muscle activity. Another element to consider is the necessity to regulate airflow without creating unwanted engagement in the intrinsic laryngeal muscles by too little or too much subglottal air pressure. There is a constant negotiation between the respiration and phonation systems, influenced by pitch, volume, the quality of sound desired, and other factors discussed within each systematic chapter.

While singers want an absolute and straightforward explanation of a breathing technique, there is a great deal of variability in breath management strategies between individuals. In other words, there is no singular correct breathing method for singing. This does not negate the fact that there is a wealth of information about breathing for singing from a science-informed approach. There are many factors that contribute to a singer's breath management, the variability of which is not yet entirely understood. What is known is that singers have a tendency toward a habitual pattern of breathing for singing and that there are a variety of strategies successfully employed (Hixon, 2006; LeBorgne & Rosenberg, 2014, pp. 38–39). Body type seems to be a contributing factor since somatotype (endomorph, ectomorph, or mesomorph) may influence aspects of respiratory function during singing (Collyer, Kenny, & Archer, 2009; Cowgill, 2009; Hoit & Hixon, 1986). It appears that a different percentage of body fat to lean muscle mass affects a singer's breath management strategy, specifically how one activates different aspects of the control of airflow.

An interesting study provided evidence that even highly trained singers with career success did not accurately understand their own patterns of breathing for singing (Watson & Hixon, 1985, p. 119). A disconnect was revealed between performance success and actual working knowledge of how it was achieved. In other words, successful performance experience does not equal accurate knowledge about breathing mechanics in singers (Hixon, 2006, p. 72). Relying on perceptual sensorial experience is acceptable if one is a professional singer, but not if you are a professional voice teacher who is paid to guide a singer's breathing technique in the course of lessons to a variety of individuals.

There is substantive evidence to explain some variability in breathing technique for high-intensity singing in opera versus belting. Due to firmer glottal adduction (closure) from the thyro-arytenoid muscle activation in belting, higher subglottal air pressure is created (Sundberg & Thalén, 2015). As a result of strong thyroarytenoid activation resulting in a longer closed phase of vibration, breathing strategies may be more passive since too much subglottal air pressure from excessive abdominal wall compression is contraindicated (Scearce, 2016, p. 162). The amount of abdominal engagement employed for classical singing can create tension at the level of the vocal folds for belting. This is a result of changes in vocal fold adduction and due to the interdependence between the respiration and phonation systems. Therefore, different breathing strategies must be considered to accommodate variability of voice production between genres.

It is important to note that an approach to teaching breath management should take into account the differences of the respiratory system as a child, an adult, and through the evolution of a senescent (the process of deterioration with age) singer. For a detailed discussion on this subject, readers are encouraged to explore *The Evolving Singing Voice: Changes Across the Lifespan* (Brunssen, 2018).

Since there are a variety of successful breath management strategies, voice teachers must understand the biological mechanics of the respiratory system as it applies to singing, allow for individuality in the coordination of muscle activity, and have knowledge of the dynamic relationship between *all* the voice systems. It is necessary for teachers of singing to have a clear understanding of the mechanics of respiration and its impact on different genres in order to translate the information during studio application.

Respiratory Facts

- The diaphragmatic muscle's normal action is to contract on inhalation and then relax to its natural resting position through elastic recoil (Hixon, 2006, p. 82; McCoy, 2012, p. 84).
- During phonation, singers may use varying diaphragmatic contraction as an antagonist during exhalation to control breath pressure and airflow; and some singers achieve voluntary coactivation of the diaphragm during phonation (McCoy, 2019, p. 124; Sundberg, 1987, pp. 31–32).
- The abdominal wall is a group of solely exhalation muscles (Hixon, 2006, pp. 31, 82).

- The rib cage contacts a larger portion of the lungs than either the diaphragm or the abdominal wall. Therefore, the amount of air exhaled as the rib cage returns to neutral (collapses) is greater than that of the abdominal wall moving inward. In other words, the abdominal wall and the diaphragm must move a greater distance than the rib cage to move an equivalent amount of air (Hixon, 2006, pp. 34–36).

- In classical singers, muscle activity in the lower and lateral region of the abdominal wall was found to be higher than in the middle region (down the center) or upper lateral region of the abdominal wall (Watson, Hoit, Lansing, & Hixon, 1989). This is most likely due to the activity of the external/internal obliques and transverse abdominus muscles. (Hixon, 2006, p. 100).

- The internal and external oblique muscles are probably the most effective at depressing the ribs due to their points of insertion, and the transverse abdominus muscles interlace with portions of the diaphragm so most likely are more effective at compressing the viscera (internal organs). The internal intercostals contraction is likely delayed in singing and significant mostly at the end of very long and loud phrases, otherwise there is potential for overpressurizing the breath and causing issues at the level of phonation (McCoy, 2012, p. 88).

- Singers successfully employ a variety of successful breath management strategies. Body type may be a contributing factor to the variability since somatotype (endomorph, ectomorph, or mesomorph) influences aspects of respiratory function. (Collyer et al., 2009; Cowgill, 2009; Hoit & Hixon, 1986).

- Due to deep thyroarytenoid muscle activity creating firmer glottal closure (high closed quotient) of the vocal folds during belting, higher subglottal air pressure is created (Sundberg, 2015). As a result, breathing strategies may be more static in the belt aesthetic than in classical singing (Scearce, 2016, p. 162).

Application of Respiration

The term *vocal gym* is sometimes used in relation to singers. Since singers are now identified as voice athletes, this is a relevant correlation. Going to the gym implies a strategy to train the body for intensive task-specific work. When singers go to the vocal gym, it is important to begin each practice session with exercises to coordinate patterns of breathing for singing. Athletes begin each daily session from the ground up: a golfer goes to the driving range to establish elements of their swing, a runner first engages in squats and lunges, and a baseball player begins throwing at a close distance before advancing to a longer distance. Singers should enter into their practice session with a similar approach.

Since respiration is the power source of the voice, it should be considered an integral component of daily preparation. Acquiring a dynamic balance between muscles of inhalation and exhalation is critical to efficient singing. Often, it is necessary to isolate different elements of a singer's breathing patterns. For example, practicing abdominal wall release separately from active rib cage expansion during inhalation may be necessary. During exhalation, it is useful to practice the abdominal wall engagement separately from the ability to delay the rib cage from returning to a neutral position. By isolating specific aspects of breathing patterns for singing, it enables better control when integrated as one inspiratory or expiratory gesture. For this reason, several exercises are introduced in order to practice aspects of breathing for singing independent of voicing. Habilitating optimal breath management develops over time and with intentional practice.

There are several kinesthetic singing tools introduced for respiration: a large exercise ball, barre3 exercise ball, Futuro Surgical Abdominal Support, Flow-ball by POWERbreathe, and an exercise band. (A discussion of kinesthetic singing tools and an approach to vocal function exercises are found in Chapter 1.) Teaching optimal breath management strategies to singers requires patience and creativity, hence the inclusion of many kinesthetic singing tools in this chapter. They are very effective at guiding the process of breath management skills until singers can acquire the necessary skills independent of the tools.

Body Awareness Exercises

Every singer must explore within their own breathing patterns challenges that could impede efficient breath management. There are numerous books on singing technique that address in detail body alignment, posture, and body mapping for singing. Please refer to the selected resources at the end of the chapter for books with comprehensive sections on those topics. The following two exercises guide the singer to begin each practice session with kinesthetic awareness of the body and its relationship to singing. *If there are any concerns about the body position required of any exercise, please seek the advice of a physician or qualified health care provider before proceeding.*

Respiratory Cueing in Application

In this chapter, there are several phrases used for cueing a respiratory action for singing:

Abdominal Wall: encases the lower torso and includes the anterolateral and posterior walls of the abdominal cavity. In medical terms, it includes several layers that cover and form the wall.

Abdominal Wall Release: reducing activation of the abdominal wall and allowing for relaxation in the torso. Inclusive in this cue is the intent for singers to allow posterior thoracic expansion, which would include the relaxation of a muscle such as the latissimus dorsi.

Abdominal Wall Engagement: implies enough muscle activity to make movement happen. This would be on a continuum from subtle to more active contraction (particularly at the end of the exhalation phase) but never to the degree of rigidity. This cue includes the important core muscles.

Rib Cage Expansion: awareness of the external intercostal muscles that contract (along with the diaphragm) and move the rib cage upward and outward creating a larger circumference in the thoracic cavity.

Buoyant Rib Cage: cueing during the exhalation phase to encourage delaying the rib cage from returning to its at rest position. Inclusive in this cue is the understanding that singers must not "keep" or "hold" the rib cage in an outward position creating unwanted tension in other respiratory muscles to achieve this.

Recruitment: meaning an engagement resulting in a negative consequence.

Core Muscles: includes the internal obliques, external obliques, transverse abdominus, rectus abdominis, pelvic floor muscles (pelvic diaphragm), gluteal muscles (they help stabilize the pelvis), and the diaphragm.

Tension: in kinesiology (the study of mechanics of body movement), tension is defined as a muscle that has been stretched tight or the force it takes to stretch a muscle. Typically, it tends to be defined as an unwanted sensation due to prolonged contraction of a muscle.

Large Ball—Stretching and Lengthening

Purpose 3–1

There is an important mind-body connection for any athlete to consider. It is essential to take a few moments to mindfully transition into singing each day. At the beginning of a practice session, it is useful to engage overall body movement to loosen muscles and joints and to initiate the energetic activity of breathing for singing (Exercise 3–1). By gently lying over a large exercise ball, there will be a sense of upper body expansion, mobility of the spine, lengthening in the torso (trunk), and a stretch in the abdominal wall muscles to encourage proper posture and alignment for efficient breath management.

A

B

Figure 3–1. A–B. Image of singers lying over a large exercise ball with arms in alternative positions.

Exercise 3–1

Carefully position the body lying on the back across the ball. The arms may hang to the side (Figure 3–1A) or over the head (Figure 3–1B). In this position, take a few slow breaths, signaling the body to release any unwanted tension during both phases of the breath cycle. Begin with a natural breathing pattern for a few cycles, then, increasingly, with each consecutive inhalation, extend to a deeper breath. After a few breath cycles, carefully roll the ball forward (in the direction of the head) and backward (in the direction of the feet) a few times, making certain to use the legs for stability on the ball. Bring awareness to any areas of the body that need to release unwanted tension. After returning to a stationary position, slowly inhale and exhale, noticing any positive differences experienced in the body's alignment. Carefully, return to a standing position and repeat a couple breath cycles to experience any positive changes. The singer should feel as if they are standing taller and that the muscles of the torso have engaged in movement. This will make it easier for the rib cage and abdominal wall to more readily expand upon inhalation.

Large Ball—Posture and Alignment

Purpose 3–2

Posture and alignment of the spine are crucial to efficient breath management. Exercise 3–2 uses a large exercise ball to aid in establishing an upright alignment (pelvis and thorax) from the sitz bones to the top of the head during seated breathing exercises. This allows the pelvic floor musculature, abdominals, hip muscles, back extensors, and the diaphragm to establish a neutral position at their midrange. In a sway-back position, the pelvic floor and diaphragm rest in a descended (inhalation) position. When in a rounded trunk position, they rest in an ascended (exhalation) position. Both positions can poorly affect respiration if prolonged by putting muscles in a too short (active insufficiency) or too long (passive insufficiency) position and hindering their ability to contract. By appropriately stacking a singer's posture and alignment, it allows muscles to operate from their most ideal, neutral position for optimal breath management.

A

B

Figure 3–2. Image of a singer demonstrating a sway back position by rocking to the front of the sitz bones (**A**) and then to a curved back position rocking to the back of the stiz bone (**B**). This will guide singers in their kinesthetic sense of moving to a neutral position for optimal alignment.

Exercise 3–2

Sit on the ball with feet firmly planted on the floor as shown in Figure 3–2. The ball should be mostly stationary and not rock forward and backward with the body for this exercise. Slowly rock the hips forward (creating a sway back) to the front of the sitz bones and then backward (creating a rounded back) to the back of the sitz bones before returning to neutral on the center of the sitz bones. Continue to rock back and forth a few times noticing the mobility of the spine and hip flexors. Return to a neutral position on the center of the sitz bones and notice the alignment of the spine from the pelvis and hips to the top of the head. From the neutral position, perform any of the breathing Exercises 3–3 to 3–12.

Respiration Coordination Exercises

Many consonant sounds come in pairs and can be classified as *voiced* (vibration of the vocal folds) and *unvoiced* (no vibration of the vocal folds). In the field of voice therapy, the *s/z ratio* is one such pairing and can be used as a noninstrumental measure of the length of time a person can sustain /s/ (unvoiced) in contrast with /z/ (voiced) by then dividing the two numbers to obtain a numerical ratio. For speech pathologists, this may be an important measure for assessing laryngeal pathology along with a laryngoscopic examination (Eckel & Boone, 1981). For a voice teacher, it can be useful in evaluating respiratory control as well as a diagnostic tool for evaluating vocal fold closure (Wicklund, 2010, p. 11). The following three exercises use unvoiced and voiced consonant pairs to coordinate air pressure, airflow, and phonation.

IPA Symbols Used in Chapter 3

/s/   *s* as in s̲it

/z/   *z* as in z̲ebra

/f/   *f* as in f̲it

/v/   *v* as in v̲ideo

/θ/   *th* as in t̲h̲istle

/ð/   *th* as in t̲h̲is

/ʃ/   *sh* as in s̲h̲ore

/ʒ/   *sh* as in televis̲ion

Sustaining Unvoiced Consonants

Purpose 3–3

Exercise 3–3 uses unvoiced consonants to explore efficient breath coordination prior to adding a voiced component. This allows singers to train active control of both the inhalation and exhalation phases of breath management without the additional factor of phonation. The exercise develops control of the antagonistic relationship of respiratory muscles for optimal airflow. It also brings awareness to the interdependence of the respiration and articulation systems by conditioning the production of unvoiced consonants without unwanted tension in the articulators. Since the tongue, lips, and jaw contribute to the resistance of airflow, singers must be mindful not to allow unwanted tension when forming these unvoiced consonants.

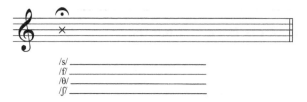

Figure 3–3. The notation for "sustained unvoiced consonants."

 Exercise 3–3

Sustain unvoiced consonant /s/, /f/, /θ/, or /ʃ/ for 10 s to 20 s (Figure 3–3). Airflow should be consistent within each exercise. During inhalation allow outward release of the abdominal wall and active lateral expansion of the rib cage. When the breath cycle transfers to exhalation, there should be a natural, subtle engagement of the abdominal wall at the outset and more intentional inward movement during the end of the breath cycle. The rib cage remains buoyantly expanded throughout the expiratory phase in order to delay its collapse. Do not forcibly "keep" or "hold" the rib cage in an outward position as this potentially creates unwanted tension in a variety of muscles. It takes time for the antagonistic respiratory muscles to develop sufficiently to achieve this expanded state. Notice the difference between each unvoiced consonant's impact on airflow. For example, how the abdominal wall engagement feels different for each consonant and whether there is a perceived faster or slower rate of airflow. The articulators should be relaxed when producing sounds.

The Abdominal Wall as the Gas Pedal of Singing

In describing the abdominal wall engagement for singers, it is useful to relate it to a gas pedal on a car. When merging onto a highway, a driver intuitively understands how to adjust energy used to depress the gas pedal at the rate of speed of the current traffic flow. If one is merging into traffic moving at a slow rate of speed, the driver does not depress the gas pedal in the same way one would when traffic is flowing at a high rate of speed. A singer makes a similar assessment depending on the needs of the upcoming phrase. Putting energy into the gas pedal is equivalent to core muscles engaging as the abdominal wall (naturally and then intentionally) moves inward while singing. This in no way implies tensing the abdomen or pulling it in. The rate of abdominal wall engagement is determined by many factors including length of phrase, pitch, volume, and genre. It is a dynamic process between the voice systems that requires consideration and a great deal of training so that sufficient subglottal air pressure and airflow are achieved. The thoracic cavity can be compared to a car frame as it *buoyantly* maintains an expansive state to help control steady air pressure and airflow. Since the thoracic cavity is in contact with a large portion of the lungs, even small movements have the potential to displace a large amount of air. Breath management is not dependent solely on the thoracic/abdominal engagement. There is a dynamic energy experienced throughout the body to be successful. Taking the car analogy one step further, the steering wheel is like cognition for singing, mindfully directing the entire process.

Rhythmic Patterns on Unvoiced Consonants /s/, /f/, /θ/, or /ʃ/

Purpose 3–4

Practicing control of the rate of airflow is an important part of a singer's training. Exercise 3–4 uses unvoiced consonants in a sequence of rhythmic patterns to coordinate the necessary abdominal wall engagement and release in quick succession. This trains mobility and control in breath management skills. The exercise also brings awareness to the interdependence of the respiration and articulation systems by utilizing the production of unvoiced consonants, which are encouraged to be formed without tension in the tongue, jaw, or lips.

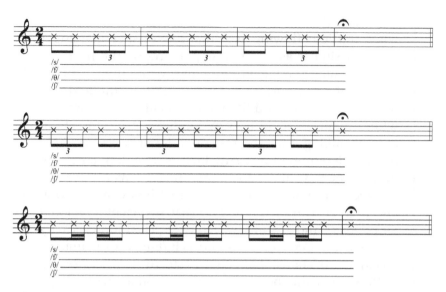

Figure 3–4. The notation for "rhythmic patterns on unvoiced consonants /s/, /f/, /θ/, or /ʃ/."

Exercise 3–4

Use unvoiced consonants /s/, /f/, /θ/, or /ʃ/ in the rhythmic patterns notated in Figure 3–4. Be certain to cue the abdominal wall toward subtle inward engagement with each individual rhythmic notation, then release the abdominal wall in between each rhythmic value notated. Alternate between the different unvoiced consonants and the different rhythmic patterns to notice any subtle changes in breath management. The articulators should be relaxed when producing these sounds.

Alternating Unvoiced/Voiced Consonant Pairs

Purpose 3–5

By alternating unvoiced and voiced consonant pairs—/s–z/, /f–v/, /θ–ð/, and /ʃ–ʒ/—singers condition the dynamic relationship between the systems of respiration, phonation, and articulation. There is a critical correlation between subglottal air pressure, airflow, and phonation that is essential to a singer's training. Exercise 3–5 coordinates these interconnections before further complexities of singing are involved. The exercise also brings awareness to the interdependence of the respiration and articulation systems by utilizing the production of unvoiced/voiced consonants, which are encouraged to be formed without tension in the tongue, jaw, or lips.

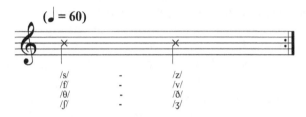

Figure 3–5. The notation for "alternating voiced/ unvoiced consonant pairs."

 Exercise 3–5

Alternate the unvoiced/voiced consonant pairs at a rate of ♩ = 60 per phoneme as notated in Figure 3–5. During inhalation allow outward release of the abdominal wall and active expansion of the rib cage. When the breath cycle transfers to exhalation, there is subtle engagement of abdominal wall at the outset of the consonant and more intentional inward movement during the end of the expiratory phase as the consonant pairs continue to alternate. The rib cage remains buoyantly expanded throughout the duration of the breath cycle in order to delay its collapse. Do not "keep" or "hold" the rib cage out as this creates tension. The airflow should have a perceived sense of evenness throughout the exercise. There should be no unwanted tension in the articulators while producing these sounds.

Accent Method

The Accent Method of breathing is a well-researched training system to coordinate respiration, phonation, articulation, and resonance. It is more well-known in Europe and often used for the treatment of voice and speech disorders, covering exercises for relaxation, respiration, and voice. The Accent Method of breathing was developed by Professor Svend Smith, a Danish phonetician and voice researcher, in the 1930s. A multidisciplinary approach to voice teaching is exceedingly beneficial. The development of exercises to facilitate efficient respiratory mechanics can be adapted across disciplines as evidenced by the fundamental principles of the Accent Method successfully used by singing teachers as well as speech language pathologists. Further exploration of the Accent Method can be found in Janice Chapman's book *Singing and Teaching Singing: A Holistic Approach to Classical Voice* (Chapman, 2012, pp. 50–62) and *If In Doubt, Breathe Out: Breathing and Support for Singing Based on the Accent Method* (Morris & Hutchinson, 2016).

Flow-Ball by POWERbreathe

Purpose 3–6

Using the Flow-ball, Exercise 3–6 assesses a baseline of airflow by using visual feedback from the ball elevation. The device provides a respiratory task to habilitate breathing patterns prior to phonation. This allows singers to train active control of both the inhalation and exhalation phases without the added component of voicing. Developing the antagonistic relationship of the muscles of respiration for optimal breath management is essential to a singer's success. This exercise also guides singers toward kinesthetically experiencing a balanced breath onset as evident by the ball elevation.

Figure 3–6. Image of a singer demonstrating "Flow-ball by POWERbreathe."

Exercise 3–6

Begin using the Flow-ball to assess a baseline of airflow by simply noticing the ball's response. The ball should neither fly across the room nor remain immobile in the base. After the initial assessment, use the Flow-ball device to maintain steady airflow so that the ball remains at about a 3- or 4-in. elevation for the duration of the breath cycle (Figure 3–6). During the inhalation phase release the abdominal wall and engage in active expansion of the rib cage as one simultaneous gesture. During exhalation be mindful of encouraging buoyant expansion of the rib cage to delay its return to neutral, while simultaneously coordinating abdominal engagement. Singers might choose to explore negative practice during the Flow-ball exercise with either too strong of an abdominal engagement, which would create hyperfunction whereby the ball trajectory is uncontrolled or insufficient air whereby the ball remains in the base potentially indicating hypofunction.

Flow-Ball by POWERbreathe

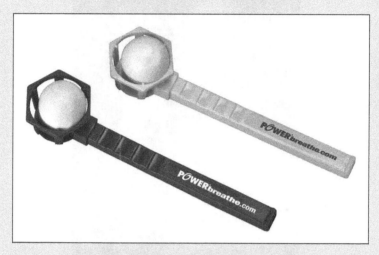

Figure 3–III. Flow-ball by POWERbreathe. Used with permission. POWERbreathe International Ltd.

Flow-ball is a respiratory device that is designed to coordinate steady airflow (Exercises 3–6, 3–7, 3–8, and 3–9). The Flow-ball device provides visual feedback through ball elevation to increase the control of exhaled air. The Flow-ball can be used to identify hyperfunction or hypofunction airflow. Singers can assess the kinesthetic sense of abdominal activity by observing the visual outcome of the ball. This chapter presents exercises that have been designed using Flow-ball to encourage a high skill level of breath management. (Note: find a carrying case to protect the ball as it easily becomes misshapen, which prevents it from effortlessly returning to the base).

Flow-Ball Voiceless Staccato

Purpose 3–7

Vocal onsets and offsets are an important aspect of breath management in singing. (They are discussed further in Chapter 4, the phonation chapter.) Vocal onsets and offsets require a dynamic control of abdominal wall engagement and release; during staccato tasks, this must be coordinated in quick succession between each pulse of air. This unvoiced version (Figure 3–7) provides an opportunity to coordinate the breathing patterns by using the ball for direct visual feedback, prior to adding phonation. The abdominal wall movement in and out should be at the same rate as the adduction (close) and abduction (open) of the vocal folds (Titze & Verdolini Abbott, 2012, p. 280). The gesture of abdominal release is as important as that to engage. (See also "Mastering Staccato" in Chapter 4, the phonation chapter).

Figure 3–7. The notation for "Flow-ball voiceless staccato."

Exercise 3–7

Blow into the Flow-ball (without voicing) at a rate of $\quarternote$ = 60 per staccato note. Repeat the pattern notated in Figure 3–7. The staccato is detached but not intentionally abrupt. The abdominal wall should engage and release at the same rate as the ball ascends and descends. It can be helpful to hold a hand above the device to encourage the ball to return to the base. Once a baseline has been established, experiment with different intended "dynamic" levels during the staccato (still unvoiced). Notice the corollary between breath engagement and ball elevation as it is coordinated with imagined dynamic changes.

Flow-Ball Voiceless *Messa di Voce*

Purpose 3–8

Messa di voce exercises emanate from Western classical pedagogical literature dating back to the 18th and 19th centuries. It requires a high level of coordination between the voice systems. As the name of this exercise implies, Exercise 3–8 presents a voiceless "messa di voce" version to separately coordinate breath mechanics prior to adding phonation. The ball provides visual feedback for singers to experience kinesthetic respiratory sensations necessary for a crescendo/decrescendo. The coordination necessary to slowly return the ball back to the base in a controlled manner is a powerful kinesthetic exercise. It is also an excellent exercise to bring awareness to high notes or *fioritura* passages (florid embellishment of a melodic line) when singers often engage breath to the highest note and then inadvertently disengage the breath connection on the melodic descent.

Flow-Ball

Figure 3–8. The notation for "Flow-ball voiceless messa di voce."

Exercise 3–8

This unvoiced exercise begins by blowing into the Flow-ball and slowly raising the ball to a high elevation before *slowly* lowering the ball back to the base, mimicking breath management of messa di voce (Figure 3–8). This should take the entirety of the breath cycle at a pacing that can be achieved without creating unwanted tension. The abdominal wall should continue to engage until the ball rests back in the cage, in fact, it is the controlled descent of the Flow-ball that provides important kinesthetic feedback for this exercise. The rib cage should remain buoyantly expanded while the abdominal wall moves steadily inward throughout the breath cycle. Immediately following the Flow-ball exercise, sing a legato phrase from current repertoire or a passage with fioritura. Singers should experience a deeper connection to core muscles necessary for a singer's breath management as a result.

Flow-Ball Voiced "Flownation"

Purpose 3–9

Although Flow-ball is designed for respiratory only tasks, there is practice-based evidence to support the inclusion of phonation while using the device. Exercise 3–9 explores phonating while using the Flow-ball ("flownation") to provide visual feedback from the ball while voicing. This encourages steady airflow and a kinesthetic sense of core muscle engagement necessary for singing. In particular, it can be useful in training a more legato line singing since there is a tangible outcome of achieving consistent ball elevation. This exercise is also useful to demonstrate a sudden lack of airflow (ball drops) due to constriction when approaching higher notes.

"Flownate"_____

Figure 3–9. The notation for "Flow-ball voiced 'flownation'."

Exercise 3–9

Begin in a comfortably low range and "flownate" a five-note or octave scale using the Flow-ball as seen in Figure 3–9. A variety of tempi are encouraged. When phonating through the Flow-ball device, the ball should not elevate above the base itself. Otherwise, voice fatigue may be experienced. Instead, the ball may bounce around within the base or slightly ascend, but not to the degree of the previous Flow-ball exercises. Repeat the exercise ascending by half-steps to a comfortably high range. Progress to "flownating" a passage of current repertoire. The goal is a kinesthetic sense of even breath energy and the ability to produce a legato phrase.

Breath Depletion Exercises

Breath Depletion Prior to Inhalation

Purpose 3–10

When coordinating inhalation breathing patterns for singing, it is often taught from an at rest position. Exercise 3–10 conditions an active inhalation after a long phrase when a singer is at the end of the breath cycle (expiratory phase) and feeling depleted of air. This is often when negative breathing patterns develop since the body is naturally responding to the sensation of air depletion. The exercise conditions both the mental and physical preparation necessary for a singer's successful inhalation.

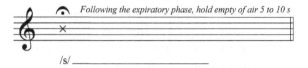

Following the expiratory phase, hold empty of air 5 to 10 s

/s/ _____

Figure 3–10. The notation for "breath depletion prior to inhalation."

Exercise 3–10

Begin with good posture and alignment. Exhale as much air as comfortably possible without collapsing the thoracic cavity; the gesture to "empty the breath" should originate in the abdominal wall not the chest or ribcage. Hold the body "empty" of air. After 5 to 10 s, allow air to enter the lungs. During the "holding empty" phase, mentally anticipate active inhalation through abdominal wall release and active thoracic expansion as one gesture (in reality, the abdominals should release just slightly before). Repeat the entire process two or three times. Then add a slow, controlled /s/ during exhalation as seen in Figure 3–10. During the expiratory /s/ phase practice actively delaying the thoracic cavity from returning to neutral by maintaining buoyant lateral expansion, while the abdominal wall gradually moves inward. Do not "keep" or "lock" the rib cage in an expanded state to achieve rib cage expansion such that unwanted tension is created.

Breath Depletion Conditioning

Purpose 3–11

The body has a natural response when running low on air. Since singers are often working near the end of their breath capacity during long phrases, this response must be conditioned. Often, singers will naturally collapse or squeeze the thoracic and abdominal cavities when nearing the end of the breath cycle. Exercise

3–11 intentionally challenges the antagonistic respiratory muscles in order to develop balanced breathing. This will train the muscles to delay thoracic cavity collapse near the end of a long the breath cycle when it senses depletion of air. In addition, the larynx is biologically an airway protector and therefore has natural patterns of protection when it senses the body is running low on air; this can be tremendously problematic while singing if unwanted laryngeal tension is created. This vocal task provides singers an opportunity to physically and mentally pattern improved breath management by emulating a common singing condition.

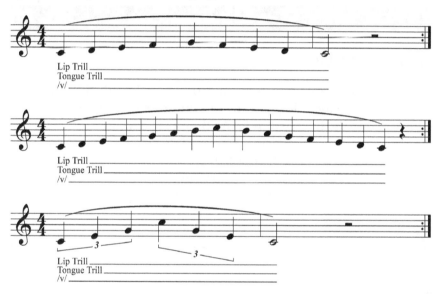

Figure 3–11. The notations for "breath depletion conditioning."

 Exercise 3–11

Use a lip trill, tongue trill, or /v/ and perform any of the three melodic patterns shown in Figure 3–11. Repeat the chosen melodic pattern until near the end of the breath cycle. Be extremely mindful of breath management patterns when the body is nearing the end of its air capacity. Discontinue singing before any evidence of visible or audible unwanted tension arises. During inhalation allow outward movement of the abdominal wall and active expansion of the rib cage. When the breath cycle transfers to exhalation, there is subtle engagement of core muscles at the outset and more intentional inward movement of the abdominal wall during the end of the breath cycle. Do not abruptly "pull-in" during the vocal onset as this has the potential of creating too much subglottal air pressure, resulting in unwanted tension. The rib cage should remain buoyantly expanded throughout the duration in order to delay its collapse.

Respiration and Resonance Coordination

/ʃum/ Patterns

Purpose 3–12 A–C

The following series builds on the previous breath management exercises while including an /m/ for kinesthetic awareness of resonant sensations. Exercise 3–12 A, B, and C explore the interconnections between the voice systems. These exercises are partially inspired by exercises in the book *The Vocal Instrument* (Radionoff, 2008, pp. 56–58). Resonance exercises will be more thoroughly discussed in Chapter 7, the resonance chapter.

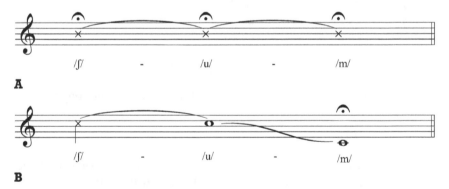

Figure 3–12. A. The notation for a chant speech /ʃum/. **B.** The notation for a descending /ʃum/.

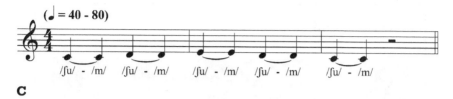

C

Figure 3–12. C. The notation for a sustained /ʃum/.

Exercise 3–12

The following exercises use the sound /ʃum/ (shoom).

A. At a comfortable pitch, slowly chant speech /ʃʃʃʃʃʃʃʃʃʃʃuuuuuu-uuummmmmmmmmm/ as shown in Figure 3–12A. Begin with a slow pace, as many as 3 s per each phoneme, /ʃ/, /u/, /m/, for the first few times. The /ʃ/ should be activated very subtly in the core abdominal wall at the onset. The /u/ and /m/ are to elicit sympathetic vibrations in the facial tissue ("mask") that the singer can associate with resonant vocal tones. Progress to a speechlike pace, perhaps 1 s per repetition of the word /ʃum/. Take as much time as necessary to coordinate each aspect of breath engagement and resonant sensations.

B. In a comfortable range, slowly pitch glide a descending /ʃʃʃʃʃʃʃʃʃʃuuuuuuuuuummmmmm/ as shown in Figure 3–12B. Repeat several times to explore the vocal range. Linger on the resonant sensations of the /m/ at the bottom of the pitch glide. The /ʃ/ should be felt subtly in the abdominal wall at onset, and the /u/ and /m/ should elicit sympathetic vibrations in the facial tissue that the singer can associate with resonant vocal tones.

C. Sing /ʃum/ on each note of an ascending and descending three-note scale as shown in Figure 3–12C. Begin at a 2-s pacing of the syllable /ʃum/ with 1 s lingering on /m/. The midrange exercise will be between C4–C5 (women) and C3–C4 (men). Practice a range of tempi between ♩ = 40 to ♩ = 80. The /ʃ/ coordinates balanced onsets with subtle abdominal wall engagement. The kinesthetic sensations of the resonant /m/ are to be encouraged throughout the exercise. Advance to a five-note scale or an octave.

Exercise Band

Figure 3–IV. Image of an exercise band used as a kinesthetic singing tool.

An exercise band may be used in a variety of ways to create an awareness of rib cage expansion or core abdominal muscle engagement necessary for a singer's skillful breath management.

Kinesthetic Sense of Rib Cage Expansion
(Exercise 3–13)

An exercise band enables the kinesthetic sense of rib cage expansion. The band can be stretched laterally in front or over the head depending on what is comfortable for the singer. This can be useful for singers with a tendency to elevate their chest during inhalation, or for those needing to condition buoyant rib cage expansion while singing. When the rib cage is already in an expanded state due to stretching the band in a chosen position, it conditions a kinesthetic sense of *breathing into a space that already exists* while singers coordinate the active expansion during inhalation.

Core Engagement (Exercise 3–18)

An exercise band can be used for singers to explore core muscle engagement. The band allows the singer to control the depth of engagement depending on how much resistance is applied to the band. Singers may wrap the band around a piano leg or step on it with their foot and then pull to create the right amount of resistance. This can be useful for singers who are underenergized or need to further explore the athleticism necessary for breath management while singing. Although the core muscles are actively engaged, they must never be rigid.

Rib Cage Expansion

Exercise Band

Purpose 3–13

The purpose of Exercise 3–13 is to actively train the rib cage expansion necessary for optimal inhalation and encourage delayed thoracic movement back to neutral during exhalation. When the rib cage is already in an expanded state, the kinesthetic sense of breathing into a space that already exists becomes more reliable. This encourages singers to naturally allow air into the body instead of sucking or gasping in air. The exercise may help singers with a tendency to elevate their chest during inhalation because expanded thoracic posture has already been attained.

A

Figure 3–13. A–B.
Image of singer
demonstrating
alternative positions
for using the exercise
band to encourage and
condition buoyant rib
cage expansion.

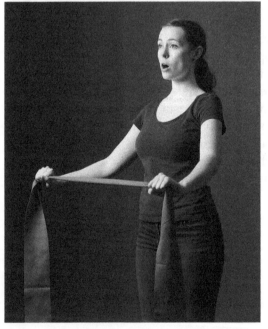

B

Exercise 3–13

Hold the exercise band over the head or out in front as shown in Figure 3–13 A or B. Choose whichever position is most comfortable and effective for the individual. Elbows may even be lower than shown in Figure 3–13, depending on the singer's tendency to unnecessarily elevate the shoulders. The expanded position of the rib cage and the slight resistance of the exercise band serve as prompts to breathe into a space that already exists during inhalation and then encourage a buoyantly expanded rib cage during exhalation. The abdominal wall should still be cued to release during inhalation and the core muscles to engage during exhalation. Choose any of the breathing Exercises 3–3 to 3–6 and practice using the band. Advance to singing challenging vocal exercises and/or current repertoire while using the band.

Futuro Surgical Abdominal Support

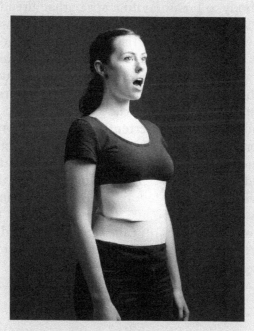

Figure 3–V. The Futuro Surgical Abdominal Support worn while singing to train a singer's breath management.

Juilliard Emeritus Ellen Faull encouraged some singers to wear a Futuro Surgical Abdominal Support. For an entire year, this belt was personally worn, including under audition dresses and performance gowns. Not a note was sung without wearing the "breathing belt." This kinesthetic singing tool was a game changer since it provided the necessary sensations to understand and condition breath management. In particular, it helped condition the buoyant rib cage expansion necessary to control subglottal air pressure and airflow. The belt is worn around the middle of the body, the top of the belt resting on the ribs and the bottom of the belt resting below the belly button. It is worn snugly so that one does not feel the need to "muscle" the ribs outward. Because of the resistance provided by the belt, it encourages the active expansion of the rib cage while simultaneously providing a reminder to release the abdominal wall upon inhalation. It also cues the body to breathe into a space that already exists (and not suck the air in), rather than muscling into the elasticity of the belt. When first learning rib cage expansion, it is important not to engage the chest or shoulders; rather, isolate the external intercostal muscles to achieve the gesture. It is common for singers first learning to actively delay the rib cage to return to its neutral resting position to inadvertently create tension in the xiphoid process area (upper epigastrium) (see Figure 3–I) when conditioning this breathing pattern. This must be monitored (see Exercise 3–15). During exhalation, the belt provides sensory feedback, reminding singers to buoyantly maintain rib cage expansion (*never* locking, keeping, or holding the rib cage open) so as to delay the ribcage returning to a neutral position, while coordinating the engagement of the abdominal wall.

Respiratory Release

Pelvic Floor Release

Purpose 3–14

There is a synergistic relationship between the pelvic floor muscles (bottom of the abdominal cavity), the diaphragm (top of the abdominal cavity), and the abdominal muscles that is acknowledged for playing an important role in breathing. Although more collaborative research is needed between physical medicine, voice science, and pedagogy to specify the role and ascertain the behavior of the pelvic floor musculature during breathing for singing (Gordon & Reed, in press), there is enough evidence to support the inclusion of exercises that explore these important connections. Exercise 3–14 encourages movement in the hip joints and core muscles (which includes the pelvic floor) in order to improve breath management that engages muscles without creating rigidity. Finding this balance is crucial for singers.

Figure 3–14. Image to demonstrate using a large exercise ball to rotate the hips in a figure eight motion while singing for "pelvic floor release."

Exercise 3–14

Sit on the ball with feet firmly planted on the floor to provide stability as seen in Figure 3–14. Rock side to side or in a figure eight motion to encourage mobility in the hip joints and core muscles. Once the singer is comfortable with the motion, continue moving in the same pattern while singing vocal exercises or current repertoire. When singers allow the hip joints and core muscles (including the pelvic floor) to be more mobile and flexible, it enables the voice to feel freer, and awareness of deeper breath coordination is experienced. The continuous movement prevents rigidity in the muscles that might prevent efficient airflow. An alternative to sitting on the ball is for the singer to stand with their knees slightly bent and move their hips in a figure eight motion while singing.

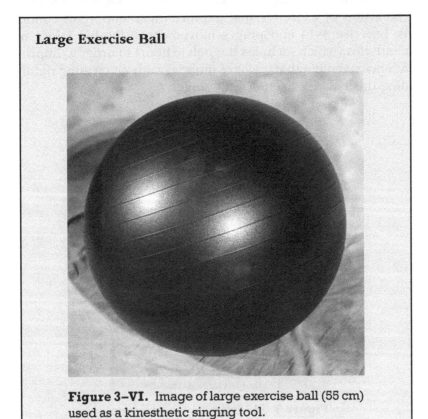

Large Exercise Ball

Figure 3–VI. Image of large exercise ball (55 cm) used as a kinesthetic singing tool.

A large exercise ball is an effective kinesthetic singing tool. It may be used in a variety of ways to encourage core engagement necessary for breath management (see Exercise 3–16, and Figures 3–16B and 3–17) or to release unwanted tension in the hips, pelvic floor, and core muscles (Exercise 3–14) during efficient singing. The 55-cm ball seems to be the best size for most singers. Depending on the exercise, the 65-cm ball might be more appropriate for taller students. The large ball exercises are useful for stretching, alignment, expansion, and engagement of the body for developing optimal respiratory mechanics.

Xiphoid Process Area Release

Purpose 3–15

The xiphoid procees (bottom of the sternum; see Figure 3–I) is a point of attachment for respiratory muscles, including the diaphragm, and acts as an insertion for the rectus adominus and transversus abdominus muscles. Tension is often held in this area, especially when singers are working toward an expanded rib cage, necessary for a singer's breath management. Exercise 3–15 encourages a release of unwanted muscle tension in this area, which is often a result of trying to "keep" or "hold" the rib cage in an outward position. By placing the ball in the upper epigastrium and leaning into it while singing, this may release unwanted tension preventing optimal airflow. Singers will notice lower abdominal engagement, a sense of more even airflow, and an overall freer sound.

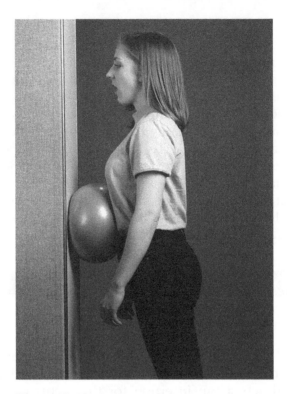

Figure 3–15. Image to demonstrate leaning into a barre3 ball while singing to encourage "xiphoid process area release."

Exercise 3–15

Place the ball in the upper epigastric region (upper abdominal) while leaning into a doorway as shown in Figure 3–15. The body should be at a comfortable angle as the singer leans into the ball and doorway. The singer should control the depth of angle, whether steep or shallow, depending on their needs. The neck must stay in a neutral alignment and the chin straight forward, not angled. While in this position, sing any vocal exercise or current repertoire. An alternative to using the ball for this exercise would be to have the singer place their fingers in the upper epigastrium/xiphoid process area and massage while singing. As a result of releasing held tension in this area, singers notice a freer, more resonant voice and often report sensations of lower abdominal wall engagement as a result.

barre3 Ball

Figure 3–VII. Image of the barre3 ball used as a kinesthetic singing tool.

The barre3 ball has a squishy quality that works perfectly as a kinesthetic singing tool. There are many exercises to explore with the barre3 ball for conditioning breath management:

Core engagement (Exercises 3–16A, 3–16C, 3–16D) can be experienced by squeezing the barre3 ball between the hands, knees, or ankles while singing. This enables singers to feel the connection to the core muscles necessary for breath management. It also tends to release unwanted tension elsewhere in their body by focusing energy where it is most useful. Core muscles must be engaged but never rigid. Practicing that balance can be facilitated by using the ball.

Xiphoid process area release (Exercise 3–15) is achieved by placing the ball in the area around the xiphoid process (a small cartilaginous process at the bottom of the sternum) and leaning into it. This area is a point of attachment for many breathing muscles, including the diaphragm.

Unwanted tension is often developed in this area, especially when singers are working toward an expanded rib cage and have unintentionally engaged muscles in an effort to "keep" or "hold" their ribcage outward. By placing the ball in the upper epigastrium, unnecessary tension may be released, and singers will notice optimal lower abdominal wall engagement, better airflow, and an overall freer, more resonant sound.

Core Engagement

Encouraging Core Engagement Through Exercise Balls

Purpose 3–16

The purpose of Exercise 3–16 is to encourage core activation (including glutes, hips, pelvic floor, and abdominal muscles) as well as full-body energy for optimal breath management in singing. The balls serve as kinesthetic singing tools to habilitate necessary lower body engagement, particularly the core muscles, which contribute to breath management and overall energetic response of the lower body necessary to be a successful voice athlete. Singers are in a constant dynamic state of breath management that includes both the release and engagement of muscles throughout a respiration cycle. When proper breath management is achieved, it provides balance to the other voice systems. By squeezing the different balls from a variety of positions, singers will become aware of subtle changes to muscle engagement and its impact on breath management for singing. Of course, singing is also a coordinated dance between all the voice systems.

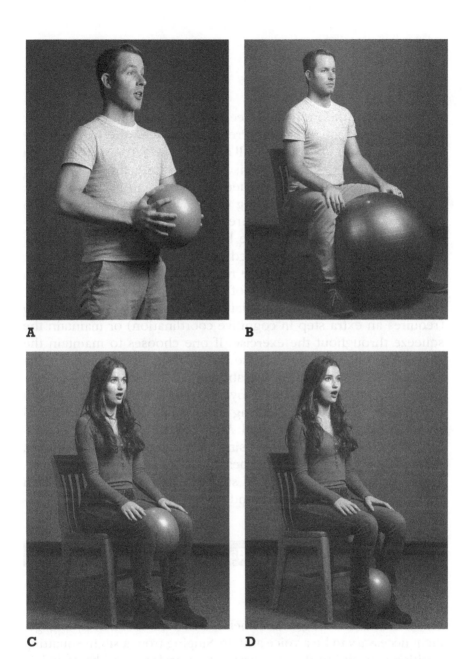

Figure 3-16. A. Image to demonstrate the position for squeezing a small barre3 ball between the hands to encourage core engagement. **B.** Image to demonstrate position for squeezing a large ball between the legs to encourage core engagement. **C.** Image to demonstrate the position for squeezing a barre3 ball between the knees to encourage core engagement. **D.** Image to demonstrate squeezing the barre3 ball between the ankles to encourage core engagement.

Exercise 3–16

Depending on the individual needs of the singer, one may prefer standing while squeezing a barre3 ball between the hands at the level of the lower abdominal wall area (Figure 3–16A), sitting down while squeezing a large exercise ball between the legs (Figure 3–16B), sitting down while squeezing a Barre3 ball between the knees (Figure 3–16C), or sitting down while squeezing a barre3 ball between the ankles (Figure 3–16D). Often, a seated position provides a more favorable kinesthetic sense of lower body engagement, including improved pelvic stability and pelvic floor engagement while singing. The results will be individual to each singer as they explore a variety of ball positions. Singers can either release the squeeze during inhalation and re-engage during singing (requires an extra step in cognitive coordination) or maintain the squeeze throughout the exercise. If one chooses to maintain the squeeze throughout the exercise (this is most popular), one must be mindful to still release the abdominal wall during inhalation. The rib cage should remain buoyantly expanded (within a range) throughout the exercise. During exhalation, the abdominal wall should be engaged but not rigid. After exploring any of the breathing Exercises 3–3 to 3–6 while using the various balls and positions, progress to more challenging vocal exercises or current repertoire. The voice will sound freer, and singers will feel more connection between breath management and a resonant voice.

Large Ball Squat

Purpose 3–17

This exercise encourages kinesthetic sensations of full-body engagement necessary to be a voice athlete. Singing from a slight squatting position is useful to direct energy into muscles of the back, pelvic floor, and legs. Exercise 3–17 helps singers condition the dynamic, athletic state of body engagement for singing. Leaning against the big exercise ball allows spine alignment to maintain its natural s-shaped curve while encouraging energy in the lower body. This exercise helps singers experience a 360° expansion in the rib cage during inhalation due to the feedback of the large exercise ball. The squat position encourages a more full-body engagement, allowing singers to experience a different connection to their breath management while singing. As a result, singers will notice a freer, more resonant voice.

Figure 3–17. Image to demonstrate the position for "large ball squat."

Exercise 3–17

Place the large exercise ball against a wall and, from a squatting position (singer determines the depth of the squat), lean into the ball with it placed in the small of the back as shown in Figure 3–17. From this position, sing vocal exercises and/or current repertoire. Be mindful that while engaging the lower body, no tension or rigidity should be created in the breathing patterns. When properly coordinated, the exercise facilitates better voice mechanics for higher intensity singing such as opera or belting. The voice should feel freer and more resonant. An alternative to using the ball would be to have the singer stand in a squat position on their own accord. This exercise is excellent for guiding singers toward the necessary full-body engagement to be a successful voice athlete.

Exercise Band Core Engagement

Purpose 3–18

An exercise band provides an opportunity for singers to explore core engagement while singing. The band allows for variability in the depth of engagement, depending on how much resistance is used. A more advanced singer could create more resistance on the band in Exercise 3–18 by moving farther from the piano leg, which would encourage deeper connectivity to core muscles. A less experienced singer might need less resistance while exploring core engagement so as not to negatively impact the voice.

Figure 3–18. Image to demonstrate the position for "exercise band core engagement."

Exercise 3–18

Wrap the exercise band around the leg of a piano (or step on it with a foot) as shown in Figure 3–18. Pull the band toward the body and notice the sensations of core engagement. Make certain no unnecessary tension is created in the shoulders or neck while keeping the elbows laterally away from the body to cue rib cage expansion. Practice any of the breathing Exercises 3–3 to 3–6 while stretching the band. Advance to performing more challenging vocal exercises or current repertoire. Some singers will find it helpful to release the pulling of the band during inhalation and then re-engage, while others will continuously engage throughout the process (most popular). Be mindful to release the abdominal wall during inhalation and to explore dynamic engagement during exhalation without incurring unwanted tension.

Summary

Breath management for singers has a long history of debate. In the 21st century, we have a great deal of scientific evidence about breath mechanics for singers. It is incumbent upon the voice teacher to study the fundamentals of anatomy and physiology of respiration (including the interconnection to phonation) in order to guide the singer toward application of those principles. While fact-based information of respiratory mechanics exists, there is a need to acknowledge the individuality of a singer's breath management strategy. It takes a great deal of time for a singer to coordinate and internalize the kinesthetic sense of successful breathing management. Voice teachers must guide singers in exploring individual breathing strategies through a variety of respiration exercises to facilitate efficient singing.

References

Brunssen, K. (2018). *The evolving singing voice: Changes across the life-span*. San Diego, CA: Plural Publishing.

Chapman, J. L. (2012). *Singing and teaching singing: A holistic approach to classical voice* (2nd ed.). San Diego, CA: Plural Publishing.

Collyer, S., Kenny, D., & Archer, M. (2009). The effect of abdominal kinematic directives on respiratory behavior in female classical singing. *Logopedics Phoniatrics Vocology, 24,* 100–110.

Cowgill, J. G. (2009). A comparative analysis of body types and breathing tendencies. *Journal of Singing, 66*(2), 141–147.

Doscher, B. (1994). *Functional unity of the singing voice.* Lanham, MD: The Scarecrow Press.

Eckel, F. C., & Boone, D. R. (1981). The s/z ratio as an indicator of laryngeal pathology. *Journal of Speech and Hearing Disorders, 46,* 147–149.

Gordon, K. E., & Reed, O. (in press). The role of the pelvic floor in respiration: A multidisciplinary literature review. *Journal of Voice.*

Hixon, T. J. (2006). *Respiratory function in singing.* Tuscon, AZ: Redington Brown.

Hoit, J., & Hixon, T. (1986). Body type and speech breathing. *Journal of Speech and Hearing Research, 29*(3), 314.

LeBorgne, W. D., & Rosenberg, M. (2014). *The vocal athlete.* San Diego, CA: Plural Publishing.

McCoy, S. (2012). *Your voice: An inside view* (2nd ed.). Delaware, OH: Inside View Press.

McCoy, S. (2019). *Your voice: An inside view* (3rd ed.). Delaware, OH: Inside View Press.

Morris, R., & Hutchison, L. (2016). *If in doubt, breathe out! Breathing and support for singing based on the accent method.* Devon, UK: Compton.

Radionoff, S. L. (2008). *The vocal instrument.* San Diego, CA: Plural Publishing.

Scearce, L. (2016). *Manual of singing voice rehabilitation: A practical approach to vocal health and wellness.* San Diego, CA: Plural Publishing.

Sundberg, J. (1987). *The science of the singing voice.* Dekalb, IL: Northern Illinois University Press.

Sundberg, J., & Thalén, M. (2015). Respiratory and acoustical differences between belt and neutral style of singing. *Journal of Voice, 29*(4), 418–425.

Titze, I., & Verdolini Abbott, K. (2012). *Vocology: The science and practice of voice habilitation.* Salt Lake City, UT: National Center for Voice and Speech.

Watson, P., & Hixon, T. (1985). Respiratory kinematics in classical (opera) singers. *Journal of Speech and Hearing Research, 28*(1), 104–122.

Watson, P., Hoit, J., Lansing, R., & Hixon, T. (1989). Abdominal muscle activity during classical singing. *Journal of Voice, 3*(1), 24–31.

Wicklund, K. (2010). *Singing voice rehabilitation: A guide for the voice teacher and speech-language pathologist.* Clifton Park, NY: Delmar.

Selected Resources

Conable, B. (1995). *How to learn the Alexander technique: A manual for singers*. Portland, OR: Andover.

Dimon, T. (2018). *Anatomy of the voice: An illustrated guide for singers, vocal coaches, and speech therapists*. Berkeley, CA: North Atlantic Books.

Malde, M., Allen, M. J., & Zeller, K. A. (2009). *What every singer needs to know about the body*. San Diego, CA: Plural Publishing.

Michael, D. (2010). Dispelling vocal myths. Part 1: "Sing from your diaphragm!" *Journal of Singing, 66*(5), 547–551.

Pettersen, V., & Westgaard, R. H. (2004). The association between upper trapezius activity and thorax movement in classical singing. *Journal of Voice, 918*(4), 500–512.

Traser, L., Özen, A. C., Burk, F., Burdumy, M., Bock, M., Richter, B., & Echternach, M. (2017). Respiratory dynamics in phonation and breathing—A real-time MRI study. *Respiratory Physiology & Neurobiology, 236*, 69–77.

Chapter 4

A Systematic
Approach to Phonation

*Voice is our primary means of expression. In combination
with our face and hands, it signals who we are, what
we want, and how we feel. . . .Throughout life, voice
continues to change, reflecting our culture, personal habits,
conditions of health, and age.*

—Ingo R. Titze, *Principles of Voice Production* (1994), p. xvii

Overview of Phonation

Phonation is the production of vocal sound. A basic overview of
the phonatory system requires a broad understanding of vocal fold
structure, principles of oscillation, and laryngeal framework. Vocal
folds (sometimes called vocal cords) consist of structured layers of
tissue: epithelium, lamina propria (superficial, intermediate, and
deep), and the thyroarytenoid muscle (Figure 4–I). Each layer has
a different degree of viscosity and density that allow the surface
(referred to as the cover) to move independently of the deeper layers (referred to as the body) (Fujimura, 1981; Hirano, 1974, 1977).
It is this structured composition that enables the vocal folds to
oscillate in a wavelike fashion, creating what is often referred to
as the mucosal wave.

Oscillation, or vibration of the vocal folds occurs due to muscle
activity that initiates adduction (closing of the glottis), biomechanics

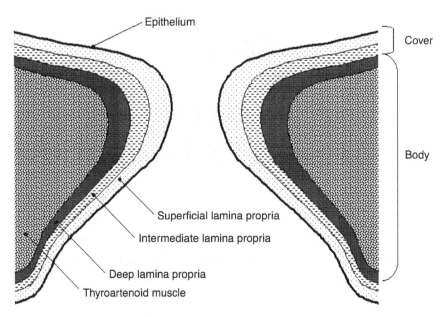

Figure 4–I. Layers of the adult vocal folds. From *The Evolving Singing Voice: Changes Across the Lifespan* (p. 189), by K. Brunssen, 2018, San Diego, CA: Plural Publishing. Copyright 2018 by Plural Publishing. Used with permission.

of the vocal fold structure comprised of elastic properties contributing to oscillation, and subglottal and supraglottal air pressures that facilitate aerodynamic activities to perpetuate vocal fold oscillation. Discussions involving the aerodynamics of voice production require a basic understanding of the Bernoulli principle. In simplest terms, Bernoulli states that an increase in the velocity of air is simultaneous with a decrease in pressure. For the oscillation cycle to begin, muscle activity brings the vocal folds together so that air pressure builds beneath the larynx. As air pressure increases beneath the closed glottis, the vocal folds are pushed open from the underside of the vocal folds due to the biomechanics of the structured layers of the tissue. As air flows through the vocal folds, velocity increases and pressure decreases (Bernoulli effect), and that along with the elasticity of the vocal folds results in the closing of the glottis until the cycle begins again (McCoy, 2012, p. 105; Titze, 1994) (Figure 4–II). The pitch determines how many times per second the cycle repeats. For example, A-440 (A4) means the

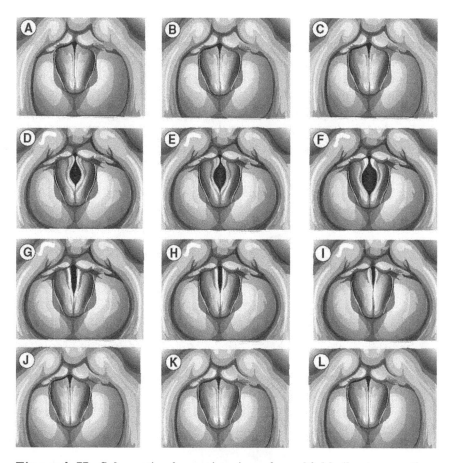

Figure 4–II. Schematic of superior view of vocal fold vibratory motion. From *Speech and Voice Science* (2nd ed., p. 140), by A. Behrman, 2013, San Diego, CA: Plural Publishing. Copyright 2018 by Plural Publishing. Used with permission.

cycle occurs 440 times per second, and a soprano high C (C6) results in 1047 cycles per second.

However, that is not the complete picture. The shape of the vocal tract also affects vocal fold oscillation due to the acoustic energy created; as sound waves travel through the vocal tract, some of the energy feeds back to the source (vocal folds) and may either help or hinder vibration. When acoustic pressures above and below the vocal folds occur during the open and closed phases of voicing, these changes in pressure strengthen a push–pull relationship that facilitates self-sustained oscillation with lower subglottal pressure (Titze, 2006). This is known as vocal tract inertance and will be discussed further in the semi-occluded vocal tract (SOVT) section of this chapter.

The vocal folds reside within the laryngeal framework, a biological structure comprised of bone, cartilage, joints, ligaments, membranes, and intrinsic and extrinsic laryngeal muscles (Figure 4–III). The hyoid bone is the point of suspension of the larynx and point

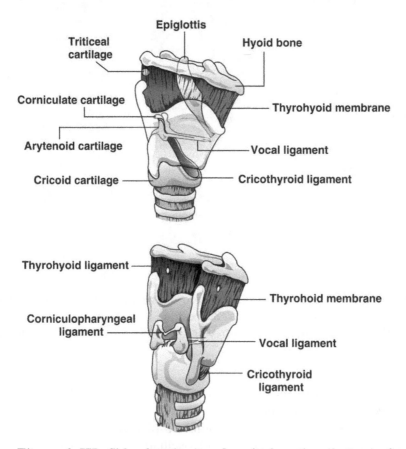

Figure 4–III. Side view (*top*) and sagittal section (*bottom*) of laryngeal framework. Adapted from *The Vocal Athlete* (p. 46), by W. D. LeBorgne and M. Daniels Rosenberg 2014, San Diego, CA: Plural Publishing. Original from *Atlas of Human Anatomy* (p. 78), by Frank H. Netter, 2001, Springhouse, PA: Springhouse Corporation.

of insertion for muscles of the tongue, jaw, and other swallowing muscles. Intrinsic laryngeal muscles (muscles within the larynx) and extrinsic laryngeal muscles (muscles of the larynx connected to elsewhere in the body) play a critical role within the phonatory system. These muscles are responsible for closing (adduction), opening (abduction), lengthening, shortening, and stiffening of the vocal folds, as well as elevating and depressing the larynx. In singing, the interconnections of these muscles impact pitch, loudness, modes of vibration, onsets/offsets, and vertical position of larynx. A key to teaching efficient singing includes knowledge of the dynamic nature within the phonatory system as well as a comprehensive understanding that by changing one part of the system, it affects other parts and the whole.

Teacher Takeaways of Phonation

Knowledge of the phonation system enables voice teachers to translate science-informed strategies into pedagogical application *and* vocal health considerations. Singers need to consider factors such as dehydration, drug impacts, reflux, poor voice habits, and overall vocal dose (the amount of time voicing) because each factor has a profound effect on the voice. For vocal folds to vibrate efficiently, proper hydration is necessary. Dehydration—either from lack of hydration, a side effect of over-the-counter or prescription drugs, or other considerations—can have a negative impact on the vocal folds' ability to easily glide across each other during oscillation. This leads to a shearing impact on the vocal folds, with possible long-term consequences. An excellent resource about medications and herbs that affect the voice can be obtained at The National Center for Voice and Speech website (http://www.ncvs .org/rx.html). Although singers must remain vigilant about their own vocal health, this information should never replace a consultation with a voice team, primarily a laryngologist and speech-language pathologist who specialize in the performing voice.

Vocal fold inflammation can occur from a common cold, virus, voice overuse, misuse, reflux, allergies, or other more serious reasons. Edema (swelling) of the vocal folds from injury, infection, or misuse may impede optimal vibration due to the inflammation of the tissue. Teachers must listen for potential vocal health concerns and recognize when and whom to refer should the need arise (Ragan, 2017). Teachers of singing should *never* conjecture any medical diagnosis. While a voice teacher's highly trained ears are often exceptional for "diagnosing" inefficiencies (technical or vocal health concerns), they must never substitute for a proper medical evaluation.

There are many pedagogical considerations for training singers as a result of knowledge of the phonation system. This includes an understanding of the significant influences on the phonation system due to growth changes during puberty and throughout the life span of a singer's voice (Brunssen, 2018). (For a substantial discussion on the influence of hormones and the female voice, readers are referred to Jean Abitbol's work in the Selected Resources section at the end of this chapter.) When voice teachers understand fundamental principles of vocal fold vibration, this leads to clarity with regards to how and why to design a vocal exercise to facilitate technical improvements. This includes avoiding negative vocal fold impact stresses, optimizing acoustic energy (vocal tract inertance), teaching balanced vocal onsets and offsets, considerations of laryngeal height, and matters pertaining to registration. Voice research has revealed that healthy voicing is achieved with a barely adducted/abducted vocal fold posture (Berry et al., 2001; Verdolini, Druker, Palmer, & Samawi, 1998). Singers can achieve this with exercises known as semi-occlusions of the vocal tract (SOVT), which are excellent at influencing low effort for vocal efficiency.

Overview of Semi-Occluded Vocal Tract (SOVT) Postures

Given that all voiced sounds involve the phonation system, one might inquire as to what constitutes specific vocal exercises within a systematic approach to teaching singing. One answer can be found in semi-occluded vocal tract (SOVT) exercises, a scientific way of referring to a partial closure of the mouth during voicing. Due to the growing body of research demonstrating improvement in vocal efficiency, SOVT exercises have become standard protocol in teaching singing. While straw phonation is the example most frequently discussed, SOVT exercises can be accomplished via lip trills, tongue trills, raspberries (tongue between the lips), fricatives (e.g., /v/ and /z/), nasal consonants (e.g., /ŋ/, /n/, /m/), hand-over-mouth, or phonation into a variety of tube sizes with the free end kept in the air (straw phonation) or immersed in water (water bubbles). The efficacy of SOVT exercises is no longer debated; both scientific and practice-based evidence exist to identify positive outcomes with regards to their impact on vocal efficiency. Extensive research has identified three significant effects from SOVT exercises: (1) vocal fold configuration, (2) vibrational amplitude and collision force, and (3) vocal tract inertance.

1. **Position and Shape of Vocal Fold Configuration**
   SOVT exercises create increased intraoral pressure (air pressure in the vocal tract) due to a narrowing of the mouth with use of a tube, straw, tongue, lips, or other means of semi-occlusion. The higher intraoral pressure (back pressure) positions and shapes the vocal folds in a parallel, rectangular glottal configuration due to subglottal (below the vocal folds) air pressure that is now more closely balanced with supraglottal (above the vocal folds) air pressure. The more rectangular glottal configuration leads to a lower phonation threshold pressure (the minimum subglottal pressure required to initiate vocal fold oscillation), prevents hyperadduction, and avoids a pressed voice quality (Guzman et al., 2013; Titze & Story, 1997).

2. **Vibrational Amplitude and Collision Force of Vocal Folds**
   Vibrational amplitude refers to how far apart the vocal folds move during each cycle of vibration. Collision force is in reference to forces applied to vocal fold tissue as they collide and is a significant consideration for singer's vocal health. During SOVT exercises, the increased intraoral pressure in the vocal tract slightly separates the vocal folds and thereby reduces both the vibrational amplitude and collision forces (Titze, 1988). Reducing vibrational amplitude and collision forces with slightly separated vocal folds allows phonation with high lung pressure and high pitch to be practiced more efficiently (Titze, 2002). These conditions further strengthen the mechanics of the vocal folds to stretch, thereby extending the singing range and providing better control of high pitches (Titze, 2018a).

3. **Vocal Tract Inertance**

Vocal tract inertance describes a condition in which increased acoustic pressure above the vocal folds during the opening phase of vibration and decreased acoustic pressure during the closing phase help to create a push–pull dynamic of the vocal folds. This facilitates sustained oscillation with lower subglottal pressure (Titze, 2006); in other words, less effort. Inertance also impacts acoustic output since the vocal tract posture either boosts or dampens the harmonics produced by the vocal folds. To facilitate sustained vocal fold vibration and amplify the acoustic output, singers want to achieve a lot of inertance at a wide range of frequencies. When singing with the vocal tract in the shape of a semi-occlusion, this acoustic inertive effect is created and therefore vocal tract resonances are lowered. The inertive reactance maximizes interaction between the vocal folds (source) and the vocal tract (filter) as sound waves are reflected back to the source, encouraging a boost in acoustic energy across a wide range of pitches (Sundberg, 1987; Titze & Laukkanen, 2007; Titze & Verdolini Abbott, 2012).

Diameter of Straw or Tube

The most frequent questions when considering SOVTs that utilize a straw or a tube pertain to the diameter, length, and material. The diameter of the straw is the most important consideration. The smaller the diameter of the straw, the greater the flow (air) resistance, which means the higher the intraoral pressure (Story, Laukkanen, & Titze, 2000). Choosing the correct size is critical to a positive outcome. Singers may want to begin with a 6-mm straw (drinking size) and, over time (one session to a few months), move to a 3 to 4-mm straw. Two small 3 to 4-mm straws work well during the transition (Figure 4–IV). One study noted that the larger 6-mm straw provided more stability in men than women (Maxfield, Titze, Hunter, & Kapsner-Smith, 2014). This outcome may be explained by the different dimensions between the male and female vocal tract and glottis. It appears that the resistance to the airflow provided by the semi-occlusion must be at a level similar to that produced by the glottis. Anecdotally, most women progress to a smaller 3 to

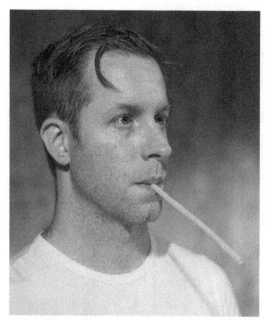

A

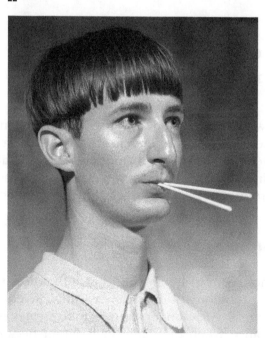

B

Figure 4–IV. Images of 6-mm drinking straw (**A**), two 3 to 4-mm straw (**B**), and one 3 to 4-mm straw (**C**) used in straw phonation. *continues*

C

Figure 4–IV. *continued*

4-mm straw while men continue to use the larger 6-mm straw to achieve the desired outcome. Singers are advised to carry a variety of straw diameters since voice demands and voice quality vary from day to day. Singers must implement daily self-assessment to determine the appropriate size of the straw needed each practice session.

Length of Straw or Tube

There does not seem to be a significant difference in the length of the straw or tube on vocal efficiency (Mills, Rivedal, DeMorett, Maples, & Jiang, 2018). A longer straw or tube creates slightly more acoustic inertance when the diameter is larger because the flow resistance occurs at both the entry and partially throughout the implement. However, because the straw already creates a semi-occluded vocal tract, the effect is negligible (Titze, 2018a). In a narrow straw, there is so much resistance created just from airflow entering the straw that resistance along the length of the straw makes little difference.

Material of Straw or Tube

A discussion about the straw or tube material centers around scientific evidence, hygiene, convenience, and personal preference. Glass, metal, and plastic tubes all have greater wall stiffness than the soft tissue within the vocal tract, so these materials do not produce or absorb much energy (Titze, 2018a). Therefore, the material of the tube matters very little. For purposes of hygiene, some singers prefer glass or metal tubes since they can be washed. The challenge with glass tubes is that the material is more fragile, less convenient, and more expensive. For environmental considerations, compostable straws could be considered. It must be noted that the sensory experience of sympathetic vibrations alters as a result of the various material. The singer's perception of the sensory feedback will help guide the selection. Plastic straws are becoming outlawed in some U.S. cities, which means an alternative plan may be inevitable. Until that time, they remain the most accessible and this author's preferred option.

Straw or Tube in Water (Water Bubble Phonation)

Resonance tube phonation in water, sometimes called water bubble phonation or cup bubbles, is an SOVT vocal exercise that was first introduced as a method for voice therapy by Antti Sovijärvi in 1965 (Enflo, Sundberg, Romedahl, & McAllister, 2013). By submerging one end of a tube in the water while voicing through the other end, a semi-occlusion is achieved. As with other SOVT exercises, phonating with a tube immersed in water creates high flow resistance, which leads to an increase in intraoral pressure and, therefore, a decrease in phonation threshold pressure. The deeper the immersion in water, the more flow resistance increases (Wistbacka et al., 2018). One study compared a glass resonance tube (RT) and silicone Lax Vox tube (LVT) while submerged in water. The researchers observed that flow resistance differed slightly (lower with LVT than with RT) and that high intraoral pressure oscillation with LVT immersed in 2 cm of water may offer stronger massage effect on the vocal folds (Tyrmi, Radolf, Horáček, & Laukkanen, 2017). Although scientific observation offered slight differences, singer's varying sensory feedback was an important consideration.

Another study noted significantly increased collision threshold pressure (CTP; the minimal pressure required to initiate vocal fold collision). Although the reason is not clearly understood, a plausible explanation is the potential for biomechanical property changes on the vocal tract walls, including the vocal folds, due to the pulsating intraoral pressure changes (static and oscillating components of back pressure) from the water bubbles that may have a massagelike effect (Enflo, Sundberg, Romendahl, & McAllistera, 2013). According to this study, a resonance tube in water also tended to cause audible improvement of perceived voice quality as evidenced by perceptual ratings of expert listeners. In particular, singers who either did not practice singing daily or those who were rated as less experienced had a more pronounced improved perceptual effect.

Although Titze has not yet studied the effect of the bubbles from water immersion in reference to laryngeal function, he states, "the unsteadiness of the pressure associated with the air bubbles does propagate to the larynx, producing a low-frequency modulation that may, or may not, have therapeutic value" (Titze, 2018a).

The studies that have researched the effects of water immersion on the voice tend to use a larger diameter tube, between 8 and 12 mm. While the larger-diameter tube still lengthens the vocal tract, it offers no air resistance by itself when voicing. By placing one end in water, singers receive the benefits of SOVT exercises due to the weight of the water, while still allowing a larger mouth opening necessary for singing. Gaining the benefits of SOVT exercises with a mouth shape closer to that needed for singing makes water bubbles an excellent tool in the voice studio. Practice-based experience and singer feedback make water bubbles one of this author's favorite SOVT exercises.

A singer's self-perception of vocal well-being cannot be underestimated. It is commonly reported that there is a sensation of a laryngeal massage effect immediately following water bubble vocal exercises. The sensory feedback reveals that the larynx feels more relaxed, which may indicate lower vocal effort and thereby improve efficiency in their singing. The production of the water bubbles is also extremely useful in providing a singer with audible and visual feedback. This is helpful in assessing vocal production and exploring the vital dynamic between the systems of respiration and phonation.

Hardware stores have an excellent supply of flexible silicone tubes with a variety of diameter options. Guided by the above-mentioned studies, begin with approximately a 9-mm diameter silicone tube cut at 10 to 12 in. in length. The depth of immersion in the water will vary depending on the diameter of the tube and the singer's individual needs. A water depth of 1 to 3 in. seems to be a viable starting point with potential modification to deeper or shallower immersion based on the singer's feedback. A water depth that does not produce excessive resistance is desired, yet the tube or straw must be immersed to some degree to receive the benefits. The advantage of making a purchase from a hardware store is that the tube may be individually cut at a longer length than that of a typical straw. The longer length tube is often easier to navigate in the water bottle. Most importantly, the longer tube encourages proper neck alignment and posture while performing water bubbles, whereas with a shorter straw, singers may tend to pull their neck to a forward, misaligned position. A water bottle or container that is narrower at the top than the bottom and that is only half-full of water is best for practical reasons. A larger diameter straw such as a regular drinking size or even larger bubble tea straw may also be used. The choice of straw will require alterations in the depth of water immersion as a result of the diameter.

Semi-Occluded Vocal Tract (SOVT) Exercises

- Position and shape the vocal folds for efficient voicing
- Encourage balanced vocal onsets (gentle adduction) and discourage hard glottal onsets (forceful and abrupt closure)
- Prevent vocal fold hyperadduction (squeezing too firmly together)
- Provide a sensation of having had a laryngeal massage

- Create stability in laryngeal height, neither unnecessarily raised (elevated) or lowered (depressed)
- Elicit sensorial feedback of sympathetic vibrations of facial tissue, which singers associate with voice production that optimizes a resonant vocal tone
- Encourage an intermediate state of adduction that leads to a lower phonation threshold pressure; this aids in developing "mixed" registration as a baseline of sound production from which to build on
- Maximize acoustic energy while minimizing vocal fold collision force
- Aid in training register transitions and expanding the vocal range

The Use of an Anesthesia Mask to Facilitate an SOVT Posture

An anesthesia mask is another option for facilitating a semi-occluded vocal tract posture (Figure 4–V). The benefit of an anesthesia mask is that it allows singers to use connected speech, something not afforded by a straw or tube. The anesthesia mask provides a firm seal around the nose and mouth, and the fingers (or palm) placed over the opening of the mask provide a great deal of control in the amount of occlusion that can be achieved. Singers may place their fingers over the mask opening and spread them to the degree needed to comfortably create the occlusion; this additionally allows for the singer to inhale without the need to move the hand. A recent study using anesthesia (ventilation) masks to ascertain benefits with dysphonic subjects and normal voice subjects concluded that immediate positive effects could be produced by connected speech phonatory tasks (Frisancho et al., in press). The ventilation mask seemed to produce a more efficient phonation and easy voice production.

Anecdotally, this author has used the ventilation mask with singers and thus far garnered mostly positive feedback. Some singers perceive extreme benefits and others are uncertain. As more practice-based evidence is acquired, the anticipation is that it becomes a regular tool in the studio since it enables the production

A

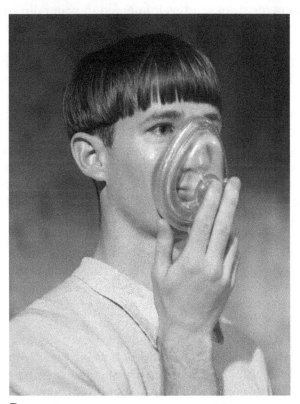

B

Figure 4–V. Image of a ventilation mask used as tool to facilitate a semi-occluded vocal tract posture (**A**), and a singer demonstrating the placement of the fingers to aid in creating the appropriate SOVT posture (**B**).

of connected speech while gaining the benefits of an SOVT posture. This will better replicate the practice of singing repertoire. The masks may be purchased at various online resources. The medium size anesthesia mask seems to fit most adult singers.

Teacher Takeaways of SOVT Postures

SOVT exercises promote a change in the system of phonation, remembering, of course, the complex and dynamic interconnection between all of the systems. To change one part of the system affects other parts and the whole. There are several SOVT exercises using various diameter straws, tubes immersed in water, lip trills, tongue trills, raspberries, fricatives (e.g., /v/ and /z/), and nasal consonants (e.g., /ŋ/, /n/, /m/). SOVT exercises vary in terms of the amount of intraoral pressure they create in the vocal tract. High-pressure SOVTs include narrow straw phonation, water bubbles, lip trills, and raspberries. If pressed phonation is an issue, then a higher pressure SOVT may be advantageous to prevent hyperadduction of the vocal folds. On the other end of the spectrum, nasal consonants are a relatively low pressure SOVT but encourage a kinesthetic sense of resonance. Even a lower pressure SOVT still provides the benefit of increased vocal tract inertance. Voiced fricatives such as /v/ and /z/ fall somewhere in between (Maxfield et al., 2014). Teachers must understand the individual needs of each singer and potential outcomes of the various SOVT postures.

Within a systematic approach, there is a natural segue to selecting a particular SOVT exercise for studio application. Singers needing detailed attention to the system of respiration might choose lip trills, tongue trills, raspberries, and water bubbles. Proper production of those SOVT exercises requires increased breath energy in order to keep both sources of vibration (vocal folds and semi-occlusion) oscillating. Voiced fricatives, such as /v/ and /z/ are also beneficial in developing optimal breath management because of the sensation of abdominal wall engagement to produce those sounds. Since SOVT exercises "position" and "square" the vocal folds in a parallel glottal configuration, this vibratory mode should be considered essential for teaching efficient singing. In particular, the higher intraoral pressure SOVTs, such as a straw or water bubbles, are excellent for training an intermediate state of adduction that leads to a baseline of functional singing technique. SOVT exercises to consider for the articulation system are tongue trills and raspberries as they are effective at eliminating unwanted tongue tension. A specific focus within the resonance system would include SOVT nasal continuants /m/, /n/, and /ŋ/ since they elicit sympathetic vibrations for the kinesthetic experience of resonant vocal tones. Even though /m/, /n/, and /ŋ/ produce low intraoral pressure as compared to other SOVT exercises, they can be extremely beneficial due to the sensory feedback they provide through sympathetic vibrations in the facial tissue (mask). SOVT exercises have many applications including resetting the voice to neutral after a heavy singing dose (Ragan, 2016, 2018) and are an essential feature of many voice therapy approaches (Kapsner-Smith, Hunter, Kirkham, Cox, & Titze, 2015).

SOVT exercises are not a one-size-fits-all, nor are they a magic fix. Like any vocal exercise, SOVTs' potential to work is contingent upon the intention of the exercise, the instruction provided, and the singer's understanding and implementation to produce the desired outcome. They can be transformative in training a functional singing technique but must be approached with caution until properly produced. There are even times when the higher intraoral pressure produced by a small straw or water bubbles is contraindicated (see the text box "A Cautionary Tale" later in this chapter). As always, a safe and communicative environment between the teacher and the student must be developed in order to ascertain whether a specific exercise is achieving the desired outcome. There are three videos (#2, #3, and #4) found on the National Center for Voice and Speech (NCVS) website that are extremely helpful at explaining the science behind the benefits of SOVT exercises (http://www.ncvs.org/videos.html).

Straw Phonation "How-To" Basics

Like any vocal exercise, straw phonation must be intentionally introduced and practiced in order to receive the benefits. A larger diameter drinking straw (6 mm) is preferred for singers first exploring straw phonation. Place one end of the straw in the mouth, make certain the lips are sealed around the straw so that no air escapes, and begin to phonate a single pitch. While sustaining the note, plug and unplug the nose. If the sound quality changes, adjustments need to be made in the elevation of the soft palate (velopharyngeal port) for this exercise to be successful. Sometimes the increased breath pressure experienced by more flow resistance results in the soft palate instinctually dropping to provide a pressure release through the nose. This results in humming instead of the intended straw phonation posture and will not produce the desired outcome. If fatigue or unwanted tension is experienced, assess whether the singer is producing too much subglottal air pressure; the lips, jaw, and tongue are a source of recruitment (engagement resulting in a negative consequence); and/or the larynx is inadvertently elevating. Visualizing air flowing through the straw (not blowing) previous to the onset of voicing is often useful. When performed correctly, singers often report a sensation of a laryngeal massage. Once the skill is mastered, there are many applications for straw phonation.

Application of Phonation

Application of the phonation system targets vocal onsets and healthy sustained oscillation. SOVT exercises are a main focus of application in this chapter because of the enormous evidence to support their efficacy. They promote a healthy intermediate state of adduction to facilitate a baseline of voice production from which to build other dynamic modes of vibration, including high intensity singing such as belting or opera. The one deviation included in this chapter is vocal fry exercises, which are not an optimal vibratory mode as a chronic state of voicing (see the text box "Vocal Fry" later in this chapter). However, at certain times, vocal fry exercises may be used to ultimately stimulate efficient voicing, including during voice therapy (Boone, McFarlane, Von

Berg, & Zraick, 2014 and cool-down protocols (Ragan, 2016, 2018). Additionally, extended vocal techniques such as growl, grunt, fry, glottal, and scream are used within the broad spectrum of contemporary commercial music (CCM) or modern classical repertoire and require interesting and varied qualities of voice production. Learning to produce those sounds should not be discouraged. However, it is useful for singers to habilitate a baseline of a functional singing technique before employing the vocal instrument in an extreme manner.

Listening for subtle changes in voice production are a routine part of a teacher's assessment. Breathy phonation occurs when there is low subglottal air pressure combined with a large amount of airflow and insufficient glottal closure; conversely, pressed phonation occurs when there is too much subglottal air pressure, reduced airflow, and high glottal closure. For vibration to be sustained, the vocal folds must not be too widely separated or too tightly approximated. The exercises in this chapter focus on habilitating balanced resonant phonation, which is neither breathy nor pressed. SOVT exercises are an excellent place to begin this work; straw phonation pitch glides, in particular, are useful for establishing this baseline.

IPA Symbols Used in Chapter 4

/i/ as in m<u>ee</u>t (pre-diphthong)

/a/ as in br<u>i</u>ght (pre-diphthong)

/o/ as in h<u>o</u>pe (pre-diphthong)

/u/ as in wh<u>o</u> (pre-diphthong)

/b/ as in <u>b</u>oy

/h/ as in <u>h</u>op except

/silent h/ a directive to think of subtle airflow at the onset of a vowel to encourage a balanced onset and discourage a harsh, glottal onset

/v/ as in <u>v</u>at

Figure 4–VI. Image of a keyboard with pitch notation.

Straw Phonation/Pitch Glides

Straw Phonation Pitch Glides—Small Intervals

Purpose 4–1

Small interval pitch glides are a useful way to introduce straw phonation to singers. Vocal exercises become more complex with larger intervals. At the beginning of each day's practice session, an ascending/descending narrow pitch interval can be beneficial. The overall structure of Exercise 4–1 is to ascend and descend across the entire vocal range using small intervals. This allows for the dynamic adjustments of the voice systems to occur more gradually. If for any reason straw phonation is problematic, select any other SOVT posture.

Figure 4–1. Notation for "straw phonation pitch glides—small intervals."

Exercise 4–1

Straw phonate a pitch glide (using straw diameter of choice) from a comfortable low range such as C3 (men) and C4 (women). Slowly vocalize an ascending pitch glide of approximately a 5th interval followed by a descending 3rd interval as shown in Figure 4–1. Continue in this ascending/descending pattern to around F4 (men) and F5 (women) before returning to the starting pitch. When proficiency is achieved, advance to the top of the vocal range remaining in the same ascending/descending pattern. This does not need to be achieved in one breath. Do not speed up during the ascending pitch glide in the upper range. The vocal task is to be performed very slowly. This allows for the dynamic adjustments of the vocal folds while gradually gaining range toward the higher tessitura.

Straw Phonation Pitch Glides

Pitch glides coordinate breath management with the changing mechanics of the vocal folds (interplay between the intrinsic laryngeal muscles) without the precision required for pitch alterations within a scale. In particular, the ratio of engagement between the thyroarytenoid (TA) and cricothyroid (CT) muscles during pitch change impacts the thickness, stiffness, and length of the vocal folds. This negotiation necessitates a dynamic variation in breath management. Ascending and descending pitch glides, in small intervals or across the full vocal range, also allow singers to explore the interaction between the resonances and harmonics of the vocal tract (Scearce, 2016, p. 173). Pitch glides (with or without a straw) enable singers to more skillfully coordinate these dynamic changes within the systems of the voice before advancing to the precision melodic patterns.

Straw Phonation Pitch Glides—Full-Range

Purpose 4–2

There is a dynamic coordination of the voice systems when using the full pitch range (see the text box "Straw Phonation Pitch Glides" above). Large pitch glides stretch the vocal folds (first ligament, then muscle), provide dichotomy between the TA and CT muscles, then require unity between the antagonistic TA and CT muscles; encourage seamlessness through the challenging passaggi; and optimize harmonic structure for voice efficiency across the entirety of the pitch glide (Titze, 2001). Pitch glides are an excellent exercise to transition into singing at the beginning of a practice session (Exercise 4–2). If for any reason straw phonation is problematic, select any other SOVT posture.

Figure 4–2. Notation for "straw phonation pitch glides—full range."

Exercise 4–2

Straw phonate a pitch glide (using a straw diameter of choice) from a comfortably low note to the top of the vocal range and a back as shown in Figure 4–2. The goal is a seamless transition from chest registration to head registration. A reduction in breath pressure and/or volume may be needed to successfully achieve this outcome. Singers often speed up on an ascending pitch glide in the upper range so be mindful that this vocal task is performed very slowly, allowing for the dynamic adjustments required.

Straw Phonation Pitch Glides—Varying Intervals

Purpose 4–3 A–D

Exercise 4–3 A–D utilize the benefits of SOVT pitch glides while also introducing the precision of specific pitch intervals. There are mechanical adjustments necessary for stepwise scalar patterns that are different than pitch glides. Depending on a singer's individual needs, one might move directly to Exercise 4–3 C or D if the smaller intervals are rudimentary. This series increases in range, allowing the voice systems to coordinate with progressively challenging vocal tasks. As the intervals increase, the balance of subglottal breath pressure and intrinsic laryngeal muscle negotiation (primarily TA/CT) may require further consideration to achieve efficient phonation.

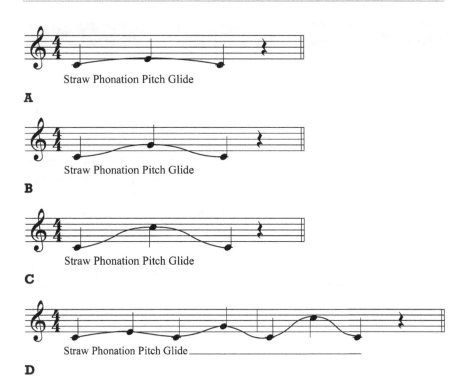

Figure 4–3. A. Notation for "straw phonation pitch glides—varying intervals" of a third. **B.** Notation for "straw phonation pitch glides—varying intervals" of a fifth. **C.** Notation for "straw phonation pitch glides—varying intervals" of an octave. **D.** Notation for "straw phonation pitch glides—varying intervals" combined.

 ### Exercise 4–3

In a comfortable low range, slowly straw phonate a pitch glide (using straw diameter of choice) on an ascending/descending major 3rd interval (Figure 4–3A), a perfect 5th (Figure 4–3B), or an octave (Figure 4–3C). Ascend by half-steps and continue the interval of choice to a comfortable middle/upper range before descending by half-steps to the original starting pitch. Advance to Figure 4–3D to combine all three intervals in one exercise. This will require particular attention to breath management strategies since it is a longer exercise across a wider range.

Straw Phonation Scales

Purpose 4–4

Stepwise scales require more precision in mechanical adjustments between the intrinsic laryngeal muscles, resonance strategy, and breath management (Scearce, 2016, p. 174). There is also a dynamic relationship between subglottal pressure and phonation based on loudness and pitch: higher pitches need higher pressure. Exercise 4–4 utilizes the SOVT benefits of straw phonation while coordinating the more advanced adjustments necessary for the pitch precision of a stepwise scalar pattern.

Straw Phonation _____

Figure 4–4. Notation for "straw phonation scales."

Exercise 4–4

Straw phonate the scalar pattern (using a straw diameter of choice) indicated in Figure 4–4. Begin in a comfortably low range (C3 for men and C4 for women). Ascend by half-steps, repeating the exercise to a high note produced with ease. Even though each pitch should be distinguished, the overall phrase is legato. The tempo, volume, and range will be individual to the singer's current needs. Since a scale is more vocally challenging than a pitch glide, a singer may choose to alternate the two before advancing to scales without glides. Progress from straw phonation to an /i/ or /a/ vowel on the scalar pattern. It may be beneficial to alternate straw phonation and a vowel in anticipation of carryover from SOVT benefits.

Straw Phonation Pitch Glides to Vowels

Purpose 4–5

Exercise 4–5 sequences straw phonation followed by a vowel-based vocal task to skillfully prepare for repertoire. This approach anticipates that the benefits of an efficient vocal setup through straw phonation will carry over when progressing to vowels. By using a descending scale and an /u/ vowel, these two factors facilitate the desired lighter vocal mechanism (vocal fold mass) for the success of the exercise. (See the upcoming text box "Mapping the /u/ Vowel".)

A

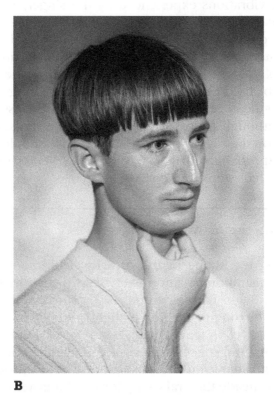

B

Figure 4–5. A. Notation for "straw phonation pitch glides to vowels." **B.** Image of singer with fingers placed in the thyrohyoid gap to provide laryngeal feedback and potential stability.

Exercise 4–5

Straw phonate a slow ascending pitch glide (use the straw diameter of choice) one octave beginning on a C3 (men) or C4 (women) as shown in Figure 4–5A. While still vocalizing, remove the straw and sing a descending /u/-/i/ vowel pattern (two distinct vowel sounds /u/-/i/) on a major scale, returning to the starting pitch. The /u/ vowel should be freely produced, with a naturally rounded mouth shape. If /u/ has any stridency to the sound, decrease volume until there is no unwanted tension, visual or audible vocal strain, or laryngeal elevation. This will be evidenced by ease of production, sympathetic vibrations experienced by the singer, and as a "tickling" of the ears to the listener. Only after efficient voice production is established should the volume be increased and the exercise ascend in pitch. It may be useful to place a thumb and forefinger in the thyrohyoid gap (Figure 4–5B) to stabilize the larynx (not immobilize or hold the larynx as it does have a range of motion). The intent is head registration for females and chest registration for males, although male voices may require a transition to head registration on the higher pitches. The exercise should ascend to a top note of approximately E4-G4 (men) and E5-G5 (women) before returning by half-steps to the starting pitch.

Mapping the /u/ Vowel

Mapping the shape of the /u/ vowel is important for head registration isolation exercises for both males and females. Begin with a neutral /u/ by speaking the word "who." The tongue position is slightly arched in the back for this vowel. Practice saying "who" several times, altering the natural speech pattern with a slightly taller internal mouth shape and oral resonance. The /u/ should feel spacious inside the oral cavity for head register isolation exercises so that a kinesthetic sense of forward and oral resonance is experienced. This is achieved by a convergent vocal tract shape (inverted megaphone), an elevated soft palate, naturally rounded lips, and a relaxed jaw.

Singers must not depress the tongue nor falsely darken the sound. A modification that allows for a taller vocal tract shape for /u/ as the pitch ascends is encouraged, especially above the secondo passaggio. When first exploring exercises to develop a light head registration (soft dynamic), singers sometimes experience delayed onsets or disruption of phonation. If this occurs, do not respond with muscle recruitment as a result of the intermittent or delayed phonation. Over time, the intrinsic laryngeal muscles will negotiate the necessary control, and, facilitated by optimal vocal tract shaping, this important skill will be acquired. It may take time to achieve a soft, floaty resonant /u/ in the middle to upper range in head registration. It is vital for singers to acquire this skill since it is at the core of developing female classical singing at louder volumes and necessary for cross-training the male classical singer. It is also a key skill for both male and female CCM singers.

Water Bubbles

Water Bubble Pitch Glides

Purpose 4–6

Water bubble exercises utilize the SOVT benefits as well as provide visual feedback from the bubbles. By observing the elevation and rate of the bubbles, singers may assess the regulation of airflow. As previously discussed, singer feedback following water bubble phonation is often described as having had a laryngeal massage. Various diameters of silicone tubes or a larger straw can be used for Exercise 4–6. Using a longer tube for water bubble exercises will encourage proper neck alignment. The depth of immersion of the tube into the water is the most important consideration: deeper immersion equals higher intraoral pressure.

Figure 4–6. Image of a singer performing water bubbles.

Exercise 4–6

Place a 9 to 12-mm tube or large straw in a water bottle. The tube should be immersed at a depth of 1 to 3 in., depending on individual's needs (deeper is more challenging) (Figure 4–6). Begin to blow air (no voicing) to create bubbles for 5 to 10 s. Assess whether the bubbles ascend to a higher elevation at the onset of the exercise (which could indicate too much subglottal air pressure) or remain constant throughout. Repeat this part of the exercise until the bubble elevation is even and breath mechanics feel coordinated. This exercise is useful to assess abdominal wall engagement during vocal onset (it should not be rigid or abruptly pulled in) and to practice buoyant rib cage expansion. Next, add voicing and perform an ascending/descending pitch glide as shown in Figures 4–1 to 4–3. The voice may feel as if it has had a laryngeal massage after 2 to 3 min. A clear water bottle allows one to assess the depth of tube immersion; however, singers carry a variety of water containers all of which can be successfully used. Singers will learn to evaluate the correct depth.

A Cautionary Tale

The laryngologist, who is the head of the voice team with whom I am affiliated, had cleared a singer to begin singing rehabilitation following a vocal fold hemorrhage. There remained a varix (dilated vocal fold blood vessel) and midmembranous swelling. During a lesson, the water bubbles were introduced and the singer reported fatigue directly following the completion of the exercise, which was therefore immediately discontinued. At the next voice therapy appointment with the speech-language pathologist (SLP), aerodynamic measures were assessed. The results determined that air pressure was normal, but airflow was increased due to the swelling (edema), which caused insufficient glottal closure. Because water bubbles and small straws (2–4 mm) create the highest intraoral pressure, use of these tools may be contraindicated at certain phases of a singer's recovery. A primary objective of SOVT exercises is to create an unpressing of the vocal folds; however, if the singer has inefficient closure, some tools may be counterproductive under certain conditions. There is variability for every singer. A singer could have vocal fold swelling and hyperadduct (press tightly) during voicing; conversely, a singer could have insufficient closure and potentially recruit in other ways. Teachers must approach every kinesthetic tool and every vocal task with caution. This is true not only for singers with a medical diagnosis but at all times, including singers' recovery from a simple cold or virus. It is imperative to ask the right questions of the singer and listen fervently to their feedback. And when there is a need, collaborate closely with a team of voice rehabilitation professionals, as in the case of a vocal injury or pathology.

Water Bubble Repertoire

Purpose 4–7

Progressing from water bubbles to repertoire is very effective at habilitating efficient voice production (Figures 4–7A and 4–7B). The expectation is that there is carryover from the SOVT benefits. Practice-based evidence supports that for this author. Since SOVTs establish efficient voicing, alternating water bubbles and the text of a song ideally sets up a baseline of functional singing technique.

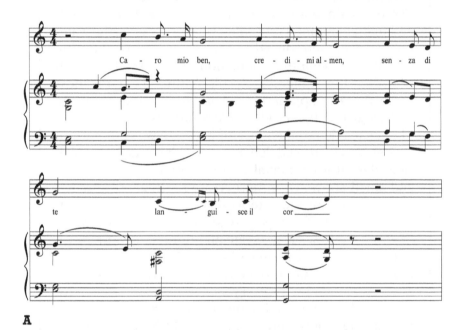

A

Figure 4–7. A. Musical selection of *"Caro Mio Ben"* by Tommaso Giordani for "water bubble repertoire." *continues*

B

Figure 4–7. *continued* **B.** Musical selection of "A Foggy Day" by George and Ira Gershwin's for "water bubble repertoire."

Exercise 4–7

Use a 9 to 12-mm tube or large straw immersed in 1 to 3 in. of water. Choose a section of your current repertoire (any genre) and use water bubble phonation to perform the melody. Work in small sections of the song, perhaps three to four phrases at a time, and alternate water bubbles and the text in the same section before proceeding. Continue in this pattern throughout the song. It is very useful to water bubble or straw phonate new repertoire when first introducing the melody to the vocal instrument. This will encourage efficient patterns of voicing from the outset.

Lip Trills

Arpeggio Lip Trills

Purpose 4–8

Lip trills have a long history as a traditional exercise to begin warming up the voice. As previously outlined, lip trills utilize the benefits of high intraoral pressure SOVTs and tend to stimulate increased breath energy in order to keep both sources of vibration (vocal folds and lips) oscillating. Lip trills are an effective way to introduce an arpeggio (Exercise 4–8) as they require more dynamic adjustments in the voice systems than a stepwise scalar pattern.

Figure 4–8. Notation for "arpeggio lip trill."

Exercise 4–8

Lip trill an *arpeggio* from a comfortably low range as shown in Figure 4–8. Ascend by half-steps and repeat the exercise to the top of an easy vocal range before descending by half-steps to the original starting pitch. Progress to a variety of speeds. It may take time to establish the breath management necessary to sustain a lip trill. Sometimes, it is useful to place a thumb and pointer finger on either side of the lips to move the area forward toward a pucker. This will help position and release the orofacial muscles for the lip trill. A tongue trill or raspberry can be used as an alternative.

Chromatic Lip Trills

Purpose 4–9

Exercise 4–9 is designed to take advantage of the benefits of an SOVT lip trill while coordinating the finer pitch adjustments of a chromatic scale. This exercise requires a lighter vocal mechanism (vocal fold mass) to facilitate seamless registration events. It further develops excellent vocal and musical skills necessary to successfully perform a challenging chromatic scale.

Figure 4–9. Notation for "chromatic lip trills."

Exercise 4–9

Lip trill a chromatic scale beginning in a comfortably low range as shown in Figure 4–9. Ascend by half-steps, repeating the same ascending/descending chromatic scale to a comfortable high range before returning to the starting pitch. Maintain a neutral larynx as the scale ascends; sometimes lightly placing a finger on the front of the larynx or finger and thumb in the thyrohyoid gap (see Figure 4–5B) is all that is needed for cueing. The tempo may be adjusted but is notated at ♩ = 60.

Vocal Onsets

Vocal onsets are an essential aspect of a singer's training. Phonation requires a dynamic relationship between the systems of voice production to initiate, sustain, and stop sound. Efficient voicing is achieved through the coordination of vocal fold closure, air pressure, airflow, and vocal tract shaping. The three types of onsets generally discussed are *glottal, aspirate,* and *balanced.* They differ in the sequencing of vocal fold adduction and airflow and in the amount of energy expended to initiate sound (McCoy, 2012, p. 113). A glottal onset occurs when strong vocal fold adduction precedes adequate airflow, resulting in a hard onset; aspirate is the antithesis as airflow occurs prior to adductory muscle activity with an outcome of a breathy sound, and balanced is when the airflow and muscle activity occur simultaneously. Broadly speaking, the ideal is a balanced vocal onset, except when considering stylistic and emotive moments within the broad spectrum of CCM or extended vocal techniques employed in modern classical repertoire. According to Melissa Cross, popular music often entails an essential juxtaposition of a repetitive rhythmic environment and the rhythm of the spoken word that must be artfully syncopated behind or ahead of the initial beat. This requires the skill of steady subglottal air pressure and airflow despite the influence of an emotionally driven emphasis (M. Cross, personal communication, June 19, 2019). For stylistic purposes, singers might choose a variety of vocal onsets for expressivity. If an alternative phonatory onset is not a chronic state of voice production, there should be no long-term, negative vocal health concerns.

When training vocal onsets, singers can choose a variety of unvoiced or voiced consonants to initiate an exercise depending on their individual needs. For example, to encourage a balanced vocal onset, choose a silent /h/ before voicing. For developing firmer glottal closure, a voiced plosive such as /b/ requires a brief buildup of subglottal pressure that can improve the thyroarytenoid engagement for firm closure. For increased resonant sensations, incorporate an /m/ or /n/ at the onset of voicing. If the focus is reducing tongue tension, use a /j/ (as in yawn) with a staccato exercise to develop independence between the systems of articulation and phonation.

Mastering Staccato

Purpose 4–10A, 4–10B, 4–10C

Staccato exercises are excellent for training vocal onsets and offsets (Exercise 4–10A–C). Staccato singing requires clean and rapid onsets, establishing a dominant mode of vocal fold vibration, and training the intrinsic laryngeal muscles responsible for opening and closing the glottis (abductor/adductor) simultaneous to the tensor muscles during pitch change (Titze, 2001). Staccato exercises provide proprioceptive feedback between the abdominal wall gesture and voicing because singers can perceive the outcome of too little or too much subglottal air pressure based on the sound quality. The abdominal wall movement in and out should be at the same rate as the adduction (close) and abduction (open) of the vocal folds (Titze & Verdolini Abbott, 2012, p. 280). The gesture of abdominal *release* in between each staccato note is as important as the gesture of abdominal *engagement* at the onset of each staccato note. There should never be a feeling of muscularly bearing down. The ability to coordinate respiratory and phonatory mechanics necessary for staccato exercises is an important aspect of a singer's training.

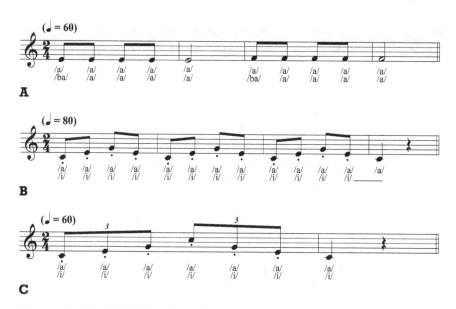

Figure 4–10. A–C. Notations for "mastering staccato."

Exercise 4–10A, 4–10B, 4–10C

Sing a series of staccato notes on a single pitch as outlined in Figure 4–10A. It may be useful to begin with /ba/ since the added consonant avoids potential glottal onset challenges while learning to focus on the abdominal wall gesture. Finding an optimal strategy for a balanced onset on a vowel-initiated word may take some adjustment since it should not be aspirate nor glottal for this exercise. Often using a silent /h/ is useful since the image of the /h/ often guides a balance between airflow and muscular engagement. This will lead to better onsets with vowel-initiated words. Cue the abdominal wall gesture to move at the same rate as the vocal onset/offset of the staccato exercise without being abrupt or aggressive. Once the abdominal engagement/release is coordinated, practice the exercise in a variety of tempi. The staccato note should onset with a precise pitch (no scooping) and be equal in resonant voice quality throughout the exercise. Progress to a triad (Figure 4–10B) and an arpeggio (Figure 4–10C). Singers may change the consonant (e.g., /m/ or /b/) depending on the current technical needs, alter the resonant strategy (classical or CCM aesthetic), or adjust the tempo.

Water Bubble Staccato

Purpose 4–11

In addition to the benefits outlined for SOVTs, Exercise 4–11 utilizes visual feedback of the bubbles from the water to train balanced vocal onsets during staccato patterns. Singers can assess the coordinated efforts of respiration and phonation by referring to the visual outcome of the bubbles. This is similar to using the Flow-ball device outlined in the respiration chapter to assess breath mechanics. If the abdominal wall gesture inward is too aggressive, the elevation of the water bubbles will be extremely high on the first note. Conversely, if there is not enough airflow, the water will have little disturbance. The arpeggio across a wide pitch range will add a layer of complexity in coordinating the voice systems.

Figure 4–11. Notation for "water bubble staccato."

 ### Exercise 4–11

Water bubble the arpeggio in Figure 4–11 using a 9- to 12-mm diameter tube (or large straw) immersed in 1 to 3 in. of water. (This can also be done with the larger straw.) The previous exercises (4–10A–C) use a smaller melodic range and can be substituted when necessary. Each staccato note should be detached but still long enough for some oscillation of the bubbles. The goal is to maintain an even bubble elevation with each staccato note in a given phrase. Repeat the exercise ascending/descending by half-steps in a comfortable range while exploring a variety of dynamic levels to notice changes in the height of the bubbles.

Staccato to Legato

Purpose 4–12

The purpose of Exercise 4–12 is to train variability needed in breath management when transitioning from a staccato to a legato phrase. The abdominal wall engagement is activated (both contraction and release) in quick succession during the staccato notes, followed by slower management of airflow needed during a legato phrase. Because of the dynamic between the phonation and respiration systems during the increasing subglottal air pressure for higher pitches, this exercise helps singers develop the necessary virtuosic breath management.

Figure 4–12. Notation for "staccato to legato."

Exercise 4–12

Sing /a/ moving from a staccato arpeggio to a legato arpeggio as notated in Figure 4–12. A silent /h/ is encouraged for the benefit of training a balanced onset preceding a vowel. This helps to avoid potential harsh glottal onsets. It is important that the rate of the abdominal wall movement, subtly but deliberately inward, matches the rate of the sung staccato notes and that there is release of the abdominal wall contraction in between each of those same staccato notes. If necessary, take a breath before the legato phrase. Because of the kinesthetic sense of the abdominal wall engagement (both contraction and release) during the staccato phrase, the singer should readily find access to the core muscles, albeit in a different strategy, during the legato phrase. The exercise transitions from quick contraction/release to a slow, gradual abdominal engagement that should be continual until the offset of the final note. Be mindful of buoyant rib cage expansion for the duration of the exercise but especially throughout the entirety of the legato arpeggio. The tempo is approximately ♩ = 110, although a great deal of variability is anticipated.

Vocal Fry

Vocal fry, also called *glottal fry* or *pulse register,* is a topic of extensive conversation due to the persistence of this speech pattern in a particular demographic of women (Parker & Borrie, 2018 Ligon, Rountrey, Rank, Hull, & Khidr, 2019). *Time* magazine devoted an entire column to the endemic use of this mannerism. Vocal fry is considered the lowest register and is "achieved with greater laxness of the vocal folds, and increased contact of the tissue" (Behrman & Haskell, 2013, p. 133). Vocal fry is produced when there is low lung pressure and airflow, complete adduction at the top of the vocal fold processes (top of the vocal folds), and low to moderate thyroarytenoid activity (Titze & Verdolini Abbott, 2012, p. 273). This causes the vocal folds to become lax, creating a loose glottal closure with an irregularly vibrating mass permitting the air to bubble through the glottis slowly. This mode of vibration produces a popping or rattling sound at a low frequency. While it is not a preferred long-term mode of speech quality production because of its limitations with regard to dynamics, timbre, and perception, there is evidence against classifying it as a voice pathology (Blomgren, Chen, Ng, Gilbert, 1998). In fact, because the vocal folds must be relaxed in this mode of voice production, vocal fry is often used in therapeutic voice protocols as an effective technique to off-load laryngeal tension (Boone, McFarlane, Von Berg, & Zraick, 2014) for vocal cool-downs (Ragan, 2016, 2018) and to improve lower notes in chest register (McKinney, 2005, p. 96). It can be used for stylistic or emotive effect within the broad spectrum of CCM or extended vocal techniques found in modern classical repertoire.

Vocal Fry

Vocal Fry—Sustaining

Purpose 4–13

Most vocal exercises are designed to condition efficient voicing. Sometimes, unusual techniques are used to acquire this final outcome; vocal fry is one such example (see the text box "Vocal Fry" on facing page.) Singers must first become comfortable producing vocal fry before incorporating it in exercises that lead to efficient phonation. Exercise 4–13 encourages practicing a basic vocal fry mode of production.

Vocal Fry

Figure 4–13. Notation for "vocal fry—sustaining."

 ### Exercise 4–13

Sustain an /a/ vowel in the fry/pulse register at the very bottom of the vocal range for 2 to 3 s (Figure 4–13). The jaw should remain in a loosely open position. The sound should be experienced as a sense of air "popping" through the glottis with no pressure at the level of the larynx. *Do not press.* Cue a dynamic contrast from piano (pp) to mezzo forte (mf) to experience the changing sensation at the glottis in this mode of vibration, then settle on the most relaxed fry register voice production without any sense of squeezing at the glottis or pushing of airflow. Repeat the exercise several times until comfortable with the production of vocal fry.

Vocal Fry to Chest Registration

Purpose 4–14

Moving from vocal fry to chest registration can help train singers to manage vocal fold mass and achieve greater periodicity (regularity of successive cycles of vibration) of vocal fold vibration (Behrman & Haskell, 2013, p. 139). Exercise 4–14 encourages more efficient glottal closure for singers with hypoadduction (airiness) and/or needing to develop chest registration. Proficiency must first be demonstrated in the middle range before moving to a higher tessitura for this exercise to be successful.

Figure 4–14. Notation for "vocal fry to chest registration."

Exercise 4–14

Produce a vocal fry for 2 s to 3 s with the mouth in the shape of an /a/. Move directly from vocal fry to an /a/ in chest registration around C4 (women) or C3 (men), immediately followed by a three-note ascending/descending scale (Figure 4–14). Ascend by half-steps and repeat the exercise, moving between vocal fry and chest registration to a comfortable middle-upper note.

Vocal Fry to Head Registration

Purpose 4–15

Young female singers often have breathy voices and need to acquire more efficient glottal closure in head registration. This can be a common condition for young female singers and patience is encouraged as natural changes occur in their growing vocal mechanism. Assuming there is no voice pathology (any concerns should have a proper medical evaluation by a laryngologist), this exercise can be useful in producing better vocal fold closure in head registration. Exercise 4–15 is designed for the singer to move from vocal fry to head registration on an /u/ vowel, specifically through the secondo passaggio in the anticipation of less airiness being produced by more efficient glottal closure.

Vocal Fry   /u/ _____

Figure 4–15. Notation for "vocal fry to head registration."

Exercise 4–15

Vocal fry for 2 to 3 s with the mouth in the shape of an /a/. Move directly from vocal fry to light head registration on an /u/ vowel at C5 (females) and descend on a five-note scale (Figure 4–15). After the singer is comfortable moving from vocal fry to head registration in quick succession, continue the pattern, ascending by half steps through the secondo passaggio to around F5. It may seem counterintuitive to move from vocal fry all the way to head registration on a C5, but this exercise can be extremely useful in facilitating better vocal fold closure. The /u/ should feel free, firmly in head registration with no stridency or pressing. The sound should be efficiently produced with forward resonant sensations. This exercise is generally designed for the female voice; however, there is nothing to preclude the male singer from exploring vocal fry to head registration exercises.

Summary

One must marvel at the glorious sounds produced by the physical process of the system of phonation. The larynx is the singer's instrument. This small mechanism is at the center of voicing. And yet, it is used extensively throughout the day to engage in swallowing, protecting the airway (e.g., coughing, clearing the throat) and, of course, speaking. It is incumbent upon every voice teacher to understand the physiological truths and basic mechanics of the phonation system in order to guide singers toward vocal health and efficient singing.

References

Behrman, A., & Haskell, J. (2013). *Exercises for voice therapy* (2nd ed.). San Diego, CA: Plural Publishing.

Berry, D. A., Verdolini, K., Montequin, D. W., Hess, M. M., Chan, R. W., & Titze, I. R. (2001). A quantitative output–cost ratio in voice production. *Journal of Speech, Language, and Hearing Research, 44*(1), 29–37.

Blomgren, M., Chen, Y., Ng, M. L., & Gilbert, H. G., (1998). Acoustic, aerodynamic, physiologic, and perceptual properties of modal and vocal fry registers. *The Journal of the Acoustical Society of America, 103*, 2649–2658.

Boone, D. R., McFarlane, S. C., Von Berg, S. L., & Zraick, R. I. (2014). *The voice and voice therapy* (9th ed.). Upper Saddle River, NJ: Pearson.

Brunssen, K. (2018). *The evolving singing voice: Changes across the lifespan*. San Diego, CA: Plural Publishing.

Enflo, L., Sundberg, J., Romendahl, C., & McAllistera, A. (2013). Effects on vocal fold collision and phonation threshold pressure of resonance tube phonation with tube end in water. *Journal of Speech, Language, and Hearing Research, 56*(5), 1530–1538.

Frisancho, K., Salfate, L., Lizana, K., Gusman, M., Leiva, F., & Quezada, C. (in press). Immediate effects of the semi-occluded ventilation masks on subjects diagnosed with functional dysphonia and subjects with normal voices. *Journal of Voice.*

Fujimura, O. (1981). Body-cover theory of the vocal fold and its phonetic implications. In K. Stevens & M. Hirano (Eds.), *Vocal fold physiology* (pp. 271–281). Tokyo, Japan: University of Tokyo Press.

Guzman, M., Laukkanen, A. M., Krupa, P., Horáček, J., Švec, J., & Geneid, A. (2013). *Journal of Voice, 27*(4), 523–534.

Hirano, M. (1974). Morphological structure of the vocal cord as a vibrator and its variation. *Folia Phoniatric, 26*, 89–94.

Hirano, M. (1977). *Structure and vibratory behavior of the vocal folds: Current results, emerging problems, and new instrumentation*. Tokyo, Japan: Tokyo University Press.

Kapsner-Smith, M. R., Hunter, E. J., Kirkham, K., Cox, K., & Titze, I. (2015). A randomized controlled trial of two semi-occluded vocal tract voice therapy protocols. *Journal of Speech, Language, and Hearing Research, 58*(3), 535–549.

LeBorgne, W. D., & Rosenberg, M. (2014). *The vocal athlete*. San Diego, CA: Plural Publishing.

Ligon, C., Rountrey, C., Rank, N. V., Hull, M., & Khidr, A. (2019). Perceived desirability of vocal fry among female speech communication disorders graduate students. *Journal of Voice, 33*(5), 805.e21–805.e35.

Maxfield, L., Titze, I., Hunter, E., & Kapsner-Smith, M. (2014). Intraoral pressures produced by thirteen semi-occluded vocal tract gestures. *Logopedics, Phoniatrics, Vocology, 40*(2), 1–7.

McCoy, S. (2012). *Your voice: An inside view* (2nd ed.). Delaware, OH: Inside View Press.

McKinney, J. (2005). *The diagnosis and correction of vocal faults, a manual for teachers of singing & choir directors.* Long Grove, IL: Waveland.

Mills, R. D., Rivedal, S., DeMorett, C., Maples, G., & Jiang, J. J. (2018). Effects of straw phonation through tubes of varied lengths on sustained vowels in normal-voiced participants. *Journal of Voice, 32*(3), 386.e21–386.e29.

Ragan, K. (2016). The impact of vocal cool-down exercises: A subjective study of singers' and listeners' perceptions. *Journal of Voice, 30*(6), 764.e.1.

Ragan, K. (2017). Understanding voice doctors: Whom to call and when to call them. *Journal of Singing, 74*(1), 53–58.

Ragan, K. (2018). The efficacy of vocal cool-down exercises. *Journal of Singing, 74*(5), 521–526.

Scearce, L. (2016). *Manual of singing voice rehabilitation: A practical approach to vocal health and wellness.* San Diego, CA: Plural Publishing.

Story, B. H. (2016, October). *Tuning vocal tract resonances to enhance voice quality.* Paper presented at the Pan-American Vocology Symposium, Scottsdale, AZ.

Story, B., Laukkanen, A., & Titze, I. (2000). Acoustic impedance of an artificially lengthened and constricted vocal tract. *Journal of Voice, 14*(4), 455–469.

Sundberg, J. (1987). *The science of the singing voice.* Dekalb, IL: Northern Illinois University Press.

Titze, I. (1994). *Principles of voice production.* Englewood Cliffs, NY: Prentice Hall.

Titze, I. (1988). The physics of small-amplitude oscillation of the vocal folds. *Journal of Acoustic Society of America, 83*(4), 1536–1552.

Titze, I. (2001). The five best vocal warm-up exercises. *Journal of Singing, 57*(3), 51–52.

Titze, I. (2002). How to use the flow-resistant straws. *Journal of Singing, 58*(5), 429–430.

Titze, I. (2006). Theoretical analysis of maximum flow declination rate versus maximum area declination rate in phonation. *Journal of Speech, Language, and Hearing Research, 49*(2), 439–447.

Titze, I. (2018a). Major benefits of semi-occluded vocal tract exercises. *Journal of Singing, 74*(3), 311–312.

Titze, I. (2018b). *Voice registration explained* [Video file]. England: Canto Webinar.

Titze, I., & Laukkanen, A. (2007). Can vocal economy in phonation be increased with an artificially lengthened vocal tract? A computer modeling study. *Logopedics, Phoniatrics, Vocology, 32*(4), 147–156.

Titze, I., & Story, B. (1997). Acoustic interactions of the voice source with the lower vocal tract. *Journal of Acoustic Society of America, 101*(4), 2234–2243.

Titze, I., & Verdolini Abbott, K. (2012). *Vocology: The science and practice of voice habilitation*. Salt Lake City, UT: National Center for Voice and Speech.

Tyrmi, J., Radolf, V., Horáček, J., & Laukkanen, A. (2017). Resonance tube or lax vox? *Journal of Voice, 31*(4), 430–437.

Verdolini, K., Druker, D. G., Palmer, P. M., & Samawi, H. (1998). Laryngeal adduction in resonant voice. *Journal of Voice, 12*(3), 315–327.

Wistbacka, G., Andrade, P. A., Simberg, S., Hammarberg, B., Södersten, M., & Švec, J. G. (2018). Resonance tube phonation in water-the effect of tube diameter and water depth on back pressure and bubble characteristics at different airflows. *Journal of Voice, 32*(1), 126.e11–126.e22.

Selected Resources

Abitbol, J. (2006). *Odyssey of the voice*. San Diego, CA: Plural Publishing.

Abitbol, J. (2018). *The female voice*. San Diego, CA: Plural Publishing.

Dargin, T. C., & Searl, J. (2015). Semi-occluded vocal tract exercises: Aerodynamic and electroglottographic measurements in singers. *Journal of Voice, 29*(2), 156–164.

Granqvist, S., Simberg, S., Hertegård, S., Holmqvist, S., Larsson, H., Lindestad, P. Å., & Hammarberg, B. (2015). Resonance tube phonation in water: High-speed imaging, electroglottographic and oral pressure observations of vocal fold vibrations—A pilot study. *Logopedics, Phoniatrics, Vocology, 40*(3), 113–121.

Guzman, M., Castro, C., Testart, A., Muñoz, D., & Gerhard, J. (2013). Laryngeal and pharyngeal activity during semi-occluded vocal tract postures in subjects diagnosed with hyperfunctional dysphonia. *Journal of Voice, 27*(6), 709–716.

Parker, M. A., & Borrie, S. A. (2018). Judgments of intelligence and likeability of young adult female speakers of American English: The influence of vocal fry and the surrounding acoustic-prosodic context. *Journal of Voice, (32)*5, 538–545.

Ragan, K., & Kapsner-Smith, M. (2019). Vehicular vocalizing. *Journal of Singing, 76*(2), 161–166.

Sataloff, R. T. (2006). *Vocal health and pedagogy: Advanced assessment and treatment* (2nd ed.). San Diego, CA: Plural Publishing.

Sundberg, J. (1977). The acoustics of the singing voice. *Scientific American, 236*(3), 82–91.

Titze, I. (2010). *Vocal straw exercise* [Video file]. Retrieved from https://www.youtube.com/watchlist=PL7dgcDJEH9K4t3YsQ78KDfjeHPN0e8q rH&v=0xYDvwvmBIM

Titze, I., (2014). Bi-stable vocal fold adduction: A mechanism of modal-falsetto register shifts and mixed registration. *The Journal of the Acoustical Society of America, 135*(4), 2091–2101.

Chapter 5

A Systematic Approach to Registration

When the teachers of the Bel Canto era noted the tendency of the voice to "ordinarily divide itself into two registers" they provided the first positive insight into the guiding principles of voice production.

—Cornelius Reid, *Bel Canto Principles and Practice* (1950), p. 71

Overview of Registration

In the field of voice teaching, a conversation about registration is a very challenging endeavor. McCoy aptly relates it to "a semantic minefield, requiring one to tiptoe through diverse, competing terminology . . . " (McCoy, 2019, p. 229). Taking labels out of the equation, an accepted scientific definition of register is a series of adjacent pitches that are produced in the same physiological manner and that share the same essential timbre (McCoy, 2019, p. 249). The important factors to be developed from this definition are the pattern of vocal fold vibration (vertical phase difference, amplitude of vibration, open and closed quotient, and length and stiffness of the vocal folds) being the same within a register and the quality of sound within the adjacent pitches having the same essential timbre. There is ongoing scientific research to explain with greater specificity the complicated topic of registration. There is still much to be understood in the context of singing that will clarify semantics in the studio. For now, it is imperative voice teachers recognize that registration is both a physiological laryngeal source occurrence and an acoustic occurrence that cannot be easily separated (Bozeman, 2013). At one time, registration was believed to be the result of only laryngeal muscular adjustments. It is now understood that acoustic factors have a prominent contribution. Timbral shifts are often a result of harmonics of the voice source (vocal folds) interacting with resonances (formants) of the vocal tract (Bozeman, 2013; Coffin, 1987). This dynamic negotiation of both muscular and acoustic adjustments is crucial to the mastery of singing.

There are many possibilities of sound quality that reside on a continuum depending on the coordination of intrinsic laryngeal muscles and resonance strategies. Speaking strictly physiologically, the two intrinsic laryngeal muscles that primarily determine vocal fold configuration are the thyroarytenoid (TA) and cricothyroid (CT) muscles, though the lateral cricoarytenoid (LCA) and interarytenoid (IA) muscles (transverse and oblique interarytenoid) also contribute to closing the glottis (Figure 5–I).

Constant interplay exists between the two antagonistic muscles (TA and CT) that has a profound impact on the quality of sound, pitch, and volume. The TA muscle resides within the body of the vocal fold. When the TA muscle contracts, it stiffens and approximates the vocal folds for broader glottal contact (Figure 5–II). This vibratory mode is used for chest registration and is often labeled Mode 1 by the voice research community. Activation of the CT muscle elongates and thins the vocal folds, creating a narrower margin of glottal contact (Figure 5–II). This vibratory mode is used for head registration and is often labeled Mode 2 by the voice research community (Roubeau, Henrich, & Castellengo, 2009).

Dynamic muscular coordination is critical to the negotiation of laryngeal source aspects of registration, whether performing within the broad spectrum of contemporary commercial music (CCM) or a Western classical genre. For training singers, the ratio of engagement between the TA and CT muscles can be conceived of on a continuum. The image of a linear slide rule is useful to explain registration, whereby the sliding central strip can be moved lengthwise toward one end or the other depending on the desired quality of sound (Figure 5–III). If one imagines the far left of the

Top view

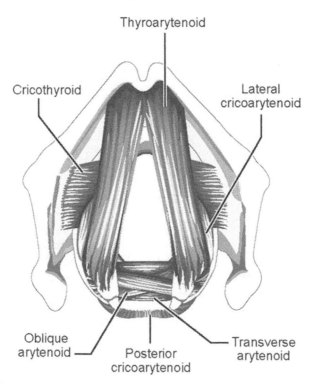

Thyroarytenoid

Cricothyroid

Lateral cricoarytenoid

Oblique arytenoid

Posterior cricoarytenoid

Transverse arytenoid

Figure 5–I. Top view of the larynx showing the intrinsic laryngeal muscles. From *Foundations of Speech and Hearing* (p. 68), by J. D. Hoit and G. Weismer, 2018, San Diego, CA: Plural Publishing. Copyright 2018 by Plural Publishing. Used with permission.

"laryngeal source slide rule" as the heaviest mechanism/chest voice quality (Mode 1) and the far right of the slide rule as the lightest mechanism/head voice quality (Mode 2), many possibilities of sound production exist along the continuum.

McCoy's inclusion of the same essential timbre within the definition of registration refers to the perceived sound quality produced by the consistently shaped vocal tract (area from the glottis/ vocal folds to the lips), which creates the acoustics of the voice.

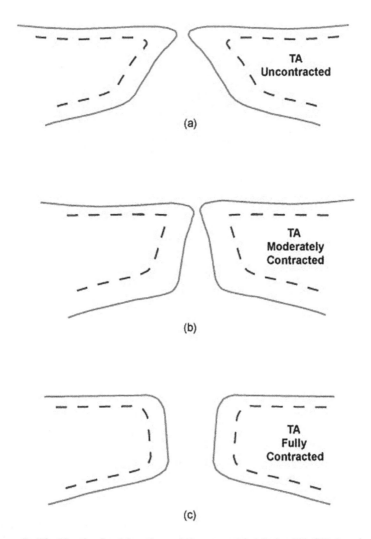

Figure 5–II. Vertical adduction of the vocal folds in (**A**) CT-dominated head register (**B**) mixed register, and (**C**) TA-dominated chest register (after Hirano, 1980). From *Vocology: The Science and Practice of Voice Habilitation* (p. 270), by I. R. Titze and K. Verdolini Abbott, 2012, Iowa City, IA: National Center for Voice and Speech. Copyright 2012 by National Center for Voice and Speech. Used with permission.

REGISTRATION SLIDE RULE

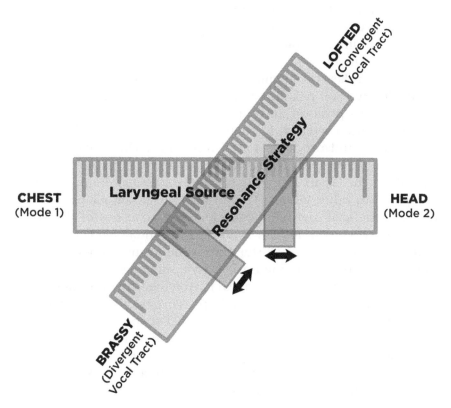

Figure 5–III. Image of two slide rules to demonstrate a continuum of laryngeal source and resonance strategy choices while singing. This visual representation demonstrates a multitude of aesthetic possibilities within a discussion of registration. The orientation of the slide rules represents the interdependence of the two components of registration: resonance strategy and laryngeal source. The resonance strategy slide rule is on a vertical plane to represent the vocal tract position of the standing singer.

Using the same image of a slide rule, moving the central strip of the "resonance strategy slide rule" to the far left signifies a brassy resonance and to the far right indicates a lofted resonance (see Figure 5–III; for a detailed discussion on brassy and lofted resonance, see Chapter 7). When the two slide rules are juxtaposed, singers can conceive a multitude of aesthetic possibilities determined by laryngeal source activity (TA/CT) and vocal tract shaping (resonance strategy). There is a broad variant of sound production options determined by the needs of the gender, genre, aesthetic choices, volume, character assessment, emotive factors, and the skill of the singer.

Western classical singing requires a longer vocal tract achieved by an elevated soft palate, a wider pharyngeal space, a neutral-low vertical larynx position, and naturally rounded lips. This vocal tract posture is often referred to as an "inverted megaphone" (convergent) shape and produces lofted resonance. The transglottal air pressure difference (pressure below the larynx is higher and pressure above the larynx is lower) in Western classical singing is lower compared to other genres. This lower transglottal air pressure is due to beneficial inertive feedback of the acoustics of the vocal tract on the vocal folds. As a result, the fundamental frequency and/or singer's formant cluster carries the acoustic energy. At the opposite end of the continuum, belt style singing requires a shorter vocal tract achieved by pharyngeal narrowing, a neutral-high vertical larynx position, and retracted lips. This vocal tract posture is referred to as a "megaphone" (divergent) shape and produces a brassy resonance. The subglottal air pressure is high due to more TA engagement, creating a longer glottal phase closure and energy above the fundamental frequency that dominates the sound spectrum. Resonance will be discussed further in Chapter 7.

Teacher Takeaways of Registration

Two primary considerations for voice teachers from research in exercise physiology are: (1) vocal exercises need to be task specific for long-term skill acquisition and (2) cross-training the instrument is necessary for vocal endurance and vocal health (this was discussed in Chapter 2). Therefore, specialized training should be a fundamental approach to developing specific technical aspects of different genres, but additionally, singers must develop the voice through a variety of sound productions. This requires practicing in both head and chest registration for vocal efficiency regardless of the primary performance genre. This is achieved through registration isolation exercises (LeBorgne & Rosenberg, 2014; Reid, 1972, p. 132; Spivey & Saunders-Barton, 2018). For example, a female classical singer who primarily sings in head (CT-dominated) registration should incorporate chest (TA-dominated) registration exercises into her training, while a female belter who primarily sings in chest registration should integrate head registration exercises into her training to adhere to cross-training principles. This encourages the development of a balanced vocal mechanism. In sports, it is an expected norm to cross-train. Not doing so would be analogous to going to the gym and working the biceps but not the triceps or the quads but never the hamstrings. There is a dynamic relationship with regard to muscle antagonism to be considered for voice athletes as well. By developing the voice in this way, the singer has an array of aesthetic and artistic sounds from which to choose; their own personal color palate. This approach supports optimal vocal health as well.

Exercises focused on the registration system are a large part of voice studio application, remembering, of course, that the systems are interdependent. A vocal exercise designed to facilitate a laryngeal source registration change (vocal folds) or acoustic change (vocal tract) will require recalibration of other parts and the whole. Registration exercises focus on making adjustments to the vibrational mode (laryngeal source) of the vocal folds on a continuum from **chest registration** (high closed quotient, increased vertical phase difference, and high amplitude of vibration) to **head registration** (high open quotient, reduced vertical phase difference, and low amplitude of vibration) and resonance strategy from **brassy resonance** (shortened vocal tract, divergent mouth shape/megaphone, narrow pharynx, neutral-high laryngeal position) to a **lofted resonance** (lengthened vocal tract, convergent mouth shape/inverted-megaphone, wider pharyngeal space, and neutral-low laryngeal position).

It is essential for teachers of singing to recognize that labels used in the context of a lesson often imply broad generalizations of a complex anatomical, physiological, and acoustic system. With regard to registration, the language of CT dominant and TA dominant can be misinterpreted to suggest that there are only two muscles involved in determining the mode of vibration for registration. In truth, there are many factors involved beyond the activation of two intrinsic laryngeal muscles. There is even research that has shown muscle activity dominance to be more related to pitch than registration (Kochis-Jennings, Finnegan, Hoffman, Jaiswal, & Hull, 2014). Some exercises in this chapter encourage activating either the CT or TA muscle, but it must be acknowledged as an oversimplification and is used solely for student cueing.

Another example of semantic challenges in studio application is the topic of mixed registration, a term that predominates CCM but is not generally used in training Western classical singers. The question often arises whether mixed registration (*voix mixte*) is a mixed-chest or a mixed-head voice production, or is it a register unto itself. On some level, singers are almost always singing on a continuum within mixed registration. There remains disagreement within the field of voice research as to whether there is a continuous progression of mixed registration or there are specific changes that require individual names (Titze, 2018). For this chapter, since no new muscles are involved and there is not yet consensus among researchers, mixed registration will be considered a variant within a continuum between head and chest registration. Although it is necessary to find a language that works in studio application, voice teachers must be careful to understand that voice production is a complicated series of events.

As previously stated, there are many controversies surrounding the terminology of registration. Some of this is due to voice scientists and singing teachers using similar terms to describe potentially different phenomena or different terms to describe the same phenomenon (Titze, 2000, p. 281). The situation is further complicated because many labels have been passed down from Western classical historical pedagogy oriented in a singer's sensations rather than function. Furthermore, due to the increased popularity of CCM, there is ongoing voice research of a broad spectrum of sound productions. This has broadened a teacher's knowledge of the principles of voice production and tremendously benefitted the field of voice. Subsequently, it has increased additional pedagogical concepts to implement in the studio. Voice teachers must be vigilant in their understanding and use of terminology.

The Broad Spectrum of CCM

Contemporary commercial music (CCM) is a term that originated more than a decade ago to replace the term *nonclassical* as an identifier for all other styles of music not considered classical. CCM is a generic term that covers a variety of music styles including pop, rock, jazz, country, R&B, gospel, music theatre, and more. Jeanette LoVetri and Robert Edwin spearheaded this important change in the voice profession (LoVetri, 2008). As teachers of singing have become more educated in the pedagogical needs of teaching all styles, it seems that CCM has become conflated with the term "belting." There are many qualities of sound production within the *broad spectrum of CCM*. Much like "Broadway" now encompasses a variety of aesthetic timbres from "golden age" or current legitimate musicals such as *The Light in the Piazza*, to more contemporary pop/rock *In the Heights* or *Next to Normal*, and everything in between. The broad spectrum of CCM is much more than belting; within the label are many genres and the potential for a vast array of vocal production and aesthetic possibilities to consider.

Application of Registration

Exercises in this chapter are designed to facilitate voice production on a continuum of chest registration (Mode 1, modal, heavy mechanism, chest voice) to head registration (Mode 2, falsetto, light mechanism, head voice). Traditional terms of *head* and *chest* register are meaningful to both classical and CCM teachers and resonate with singers in the context of lessons (Hoch & Sandage, 2017), and therefore are this author's chosen labels. The application of registration is multifaceted and requires wading through semantic challenges to negotiate a language that works between the teacher and student. Ultimately, voice studio application terminology must be user friendly and informed by principles of voice production. The exercises in this chapter guide development of a functional singing technique in both primary registers to serve as the foundation for exploration of a variety of sound production. They allow singers to explore aesthetic options to accommodate the unique physiological and acoustic needs of different vocal timbres. Knowing how to make alterations is the art of studio application. Some exercises are categorized by female and male gender to simplify notation and description due to registration considerations and passaggio events. The author recognizes that there is gender diversity. Therefore, when exercises are referenced as being suitable for the male or female voices, nonbinary and/or transitioning singers may refer to whichever exercises are most suitable for their vocal development. Vocal exercises must always be altered for the individual needs of the singer. This chapter, more than any other, requires alterations of suggested pitch range, volume, laryngeal source modes, and resonance strategies. There is a detailed explanation on the control of loudness and pitch in McCoy's *Your Voice: An Inside View, Third Edition* (2019 pp. 169–174). Readers are strongly encouraged to explore this important information. For those who teach children, adolescent, menopausal, aging, or transgender voices, there are important selected resources at the end of the chapter for further consideration.

IPA Symbols Used in Chapter 5

/a/   as in bright (pre-diphthong)

/æ/   as in cat

/u/   as in who (pre-diphthong)

/o/   as in hope (pre-diphthong)

/i/   as in meet (pre-diphthong)

/ɛ/   as in then

/j/   as in yes

/ð/   as in that

Figure 5–IV. Image of a keyboard with pitch notation.

Female Head Registration Isolation

Soft /u/—*Secondo Passaggio*

Purpose 5–1

Head registration isolation exercises are a necessary aspect of training singers to develop a balanced vocal mechanism. Practicing head registration on a very soft, floaty, resonant mode of vocal production requires the CT muscle to be more active and the TA muscle to be more passive (except for pitch control). When balance is achieved between the antagonistic relationship of the TA/CT muscles, it enables better management of register transitions, provides laryngeal stability, and permits the singer to expand the middle and upper female range in a light head registration (less vocal fold mass). Exercise 5–1 may be used throughout the entire vocal range, but the main intent is navigating the area of the secondo passaggio Bb4–G5.

Figure 5–1. Notation for "Soft /u/—*Secondo Passaggio.*"

Exercise 5–1

Sustain /u/ on a very soft, floaty, resonant Bb4 for 3 to 5 s, then descend on a five-note scale as shown in Figure 5–1. (See the text box "Mapping the /u/ Vowel" in Chapter 4.) Ascend by half-steps and repeat the exercise to a comfortable high note before descending by half-steps to a comfortable low range. F5 may be the highest comfortable note (or even lower) until singers train an efficient pianissimo head registration without any strain or laryngeal elevation in this tessitura. The vowel may need to modify slightly to a more open /o/ or /a/ in the higher tessitura; however, maintain the "bloom" of the /u/ as much as possible. This will be indicated by the singer's sense of ease of phonation and forward resonant tones as evidenced by sympathetic vibrations in the facial tissue (mask). Add straw phonation or water bubbles previous to the vocal onset if the benefits of an SOVT exercise are needed.

Sustained Head Registration Isolation

Purpose 5–2

Sustaining a single pitch on a pianissimo in head registration over a longer duration requires a dynamic negotiation between phonation, respiration, and resonance (Exercise 5–2). The intent of this exercise is analogous to a plank exercise used for core strength training. Holding a plank for 10 s requires different muscle endurance than holding it for 2 min. A soft dynamic sung in a head-dominant registration requires active engagement of the cricothyroid (CT) muscle and passive engagement of the thyroarytenoid (TA) muscle during phonation. Doing so over a longer duration optimally conditions endurance in this negotiation. This exercise is useful for female singers needing to develop this mode of voice production as a baseline of their training in order to sustain the high-intensity singing necessary for opera. It is also beneficial for teenagers, aging voices, and CCM belters.

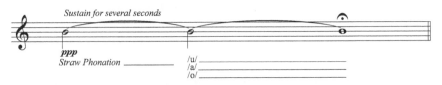

Figure 5–2. Notation for "Sustained Head Registration Isolation."

Exercise 5–2

Straw phonate the first note (around Bb4) for 2 to 3 s (Figure 5–2). Remove the straw while continuing to phonate and move directly to /u/, sustaining the same pitch for as long as 8 to 10 s on a very soft, floaty, resonant sound production. Ascend by half-steps and repeat the exercise to F5 or G5. Be certain that the /u/ is carefully mapped in its execution (see the text box "Mapping the /u/ Vowel" in Chapter 4). Cue the necessary breath management: buoyant rib expansion and abdominal engagement gradually encouraging the core muscles (without tensing or pressing) at the end of the exhalatory phase. Progress to an /i/, /o/, or /a/ vowel applying the resonant sensations of the /u/.

Turning-Over the Voice

The term turning-over is often used in training singers. It is a phenomenon that occurs in transition areas of the voice. Most often it is associated with an acoustic adjustment in the male classical singer in reference to a vowel migration necessary in the secondo passaggio to facilitate a warmer sound. Without the voice "turning-over," the sound would spread and become more "shouty." This event was historically called "cover," a term fraught with semantic debates. There is a parallel sensation in the secondo passaggio of the female voice when singing in head-voice dominated registration. The acoustic transition requires a migration of the vowel to successfully navigate into the upper tessitura so that the voice does not become thin, the larynx does not elevate, and the voice is freely produced. When correctly performed, warm, resonant tones are produced and the singer experiences sympathetic vibrations in the facial tissue (mask).

Head Registration Isolation Crescendo

Purpose 5–3 A and B

An aspect of developing balanced registration is the ability to crescendo across a single pitch (Exercise 5–3 A and B). This exercise leads to more efficient voice production throughout the range at a variety of dynamic levels. There is an important coordination between vocal fold adduction (glottal resistance/intrinsic muscle negotiation), air pressure, and airflow during a crescendo. When performed efficiently, this leads to balanced registration across a variety of dynamics. Voice teachers must learn to ascertain the correct amount of vocal fold adduction by listening for airy or pressed phonation. Once skilled at this vocal task on an /u/, it is important to practice with a variety of vowels.

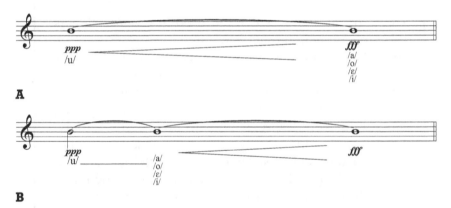

Figure 5–3. A–B. Notation for "Head Registration Isolation Crescendo."

Exercise 5–3 A and B

Sustain a very soft, floaty, resonant /u/ around B4. *Slowly* crescendo to fortissimo, making certain the voice is turned-over (see the text box "Turning-Over the Voice" earlier in this chapter) before increasing the volume. If balanced registration is not achieved during the crescendo (as evidenced by stridency in the sound or feeling of strain), slightly decrescendo to establish a lighter head registration and lofted resonance before continuing the crescendo. When a forte dynamic is stabilized, move to an /a/, /o/, /ɛ/, and /i/ as notated in Figure 5–3A. Ascend by half-steps and repeat the exercise. The vowels will need to be modified in order to achieve vocal efficiency. Success of this exercise is experienced as a stable and efficient head registration with no presence of laryngeal elevation or stridency. To the listener's ear the sound is "ringy." A variation of this exercise is to change to the /a/, /o/, /ɛ/, or /i/ *before* the crescendo as notated in Figure 5–3B. This exercise is challenging but incredibly beneficial in training a balanced registration at louder dynamics. Explore different aesthetic sound qualities once function is mastered. The desired aesthetic will determine alterations on a continuum between a slight megaphone shape (divergent resonator) for a CCM-legit sound production to an inverted-megaphone shape (convergent resonator) for a classical sound production. For classically trained singers, it is encouraged to practice this exercise at the highest comfortable tessitura, remembering to modify to an /a/ above G5.

Advanced Head Registration Isolation

Purpose 5–4 A and B

The following head registration exercises were originally designed for a classical female singer but are suitable for anyone with potential modifications to the range. Too often classical singers are encouraged to sing at a loud dynamic before the developing voice is sufficiently ready. This creates imbalance within each voice system. Exercise 5–4 A and B encourages adjustments in adduction, air pressure, airflow, and resonance strategies necessary for balanced registration in the upper tessitura by a change in volume and vowels. Classical singers will utilize lofted resonance through an inverted-megaphone shape, and CCM singers will encourage a megaphone shape appropriate for a more speechlike resonant strategy. Singers will experience more freedom and strength in the higher tessitura as a result of this exercise.

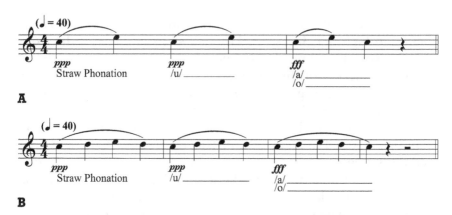

A

B

Figure 5–4. A–B. Notation for "Advanced Head Registration Isolation."

Exercise 5–4 A and B

Begin with straw phonation (or water bubbles) around C5 (or A/ Bb4 for lower voices) and *slowly* pitch glide an ascending/descending major third; continue to phonate and remove the straw while singing /u/ on a pitch glide of another major third on a soft, floaty, resonant tone; crescendo to a fortississimo and pitch glide /a/ one final major third (Exercise 5–3 A and B). Ideally, this would be performed in one breath at a tempo of ♩ = 40. Ascend by half-steps to C6 (or higher). It may take time for singers to build the intrinsic laryngeal muscle balance, resonance strategy, and breath management balance necessary for the higher tessitura (G5 and above), even when singing functionally. Even experienced high sopranos may need to pause for a moment before continuing during the upper tessitura of this exercise. The endurance to sustain a higher tessitura over a long duration outlined in this exercise may take time to develop. No laryngeal elevation should be experienced, nor should the sound be pressed, strident, or strained. Sometimes gently placing a pointer finger and thumb on either side of the thyroid cartilage (front of larynx) will stabilize a larynx that is inclined to elevate. Alternatively, place a thumb and finger in the thyrohyoid gap (Figure 5–4B; the space between the thyroid cartilage and hyoid bone) to monitor laryngeal elevation. An efficient head registration should have a ringy quality to the listener and be experienced as resonant tones to the singer. Exercise 5–4B adds a stepwise scalar pattern rather than a glide for more advanced development as discussed in Chapter 4, the phonation chapter. Alternative adjustments are to eliminate the straw phonation or sing the exercise at a faster tempo.

Advanced Head Registration—Bel-Canto Inspired

Purpose 5–5

Bel Canto repertoire for classical singers often requires an aria cadence similar to Exercise 5–5. There is a great deal of skill acquisition packed into this exercise, including staccato onsets, a slow crescendo, and a legato descending arpeggio. This is standard musical notation found in classical repertoire of the bel canto era and the exercise helps to train the necessary skill.

Figure 5–5. Notation for "Advanced Head Registration—Bel Canto Inspired."

Exercise 5–5

Figure 5–5 has several steps to consider. Begin on a Bb4 with a balanced staccato onset on /a/ before ascending a perfect 4th; sustain the /a/ and slowly crescendo during the fermata until a fortissimo dynamic, then proceed to a descending arpeggio. During the gradual crescendo, the voice must be turned-over, as evidenced by resonant sensations, and free from strain or stridency. The success of this exercise is guided by sympathetic vibrations during the crescendo and a free, easy voice on the top note, experienced as lofted resonance. Ascend by half-steps to the highest efficiently sung note in the range, potentially as high as an E6 or F6 for sopranos, before descending by half-steps to a comfortable low note.

Male Head Registration Isolation

Soft /u/ for Balanced Registration

Purpose 5–6

Head registration isolation exercises are a necessary aspect of training singers of any genre to develop a balanced vocal mechanism. When applying this cross-training principle to men, it is evident that practicing in both primary registers, head and chest, optimally conditions the voice. Exercise 5–6 encourages a seamless transition between registers within a single pattern. Adult male singers spend the majority of time singing in chest registration, the exception being countertenors and some CCM singers. Therefore, it is important to isolate and practice in head registration to develop a balanced vocal mechanism. A soft dynamic sung in a head-dominant registration requires passive engagement of the thyroarytenoid (TA) muscle and active engagement of the cricothyroid (CT) muscle during phonation. The /u/ facilitates head registration and allows a soft dynamic required for this vocal task. Head registration isolation vocal exercises will encourage male voices to gain both endurance for efficient singing in the chest voice at higher ranges as well as access to the head registration when necessary for CCM.

Figure 5–6. Notation for "Soft /u/ for Balanced Registration."

Exercise 5–6

Begin in head registration with straw phonation before preceding to the /u/ on a descending five-note scale (Figure 5–6). The quality of sound should be extremely soft, resonant, and with no presence of visual muscle recruitment or audible strain. The tone should be clear and ringy, not airy or pressed. If head registration in a high tessitura is challenging, begin a few steps lower on G4 rather than C5, then gradually ascend by half-steps until arriving at C5. This may take several lessons for male voices unfamiliar with head registration isolation exercises, especially at a soft dynamic. Repeat the exercise, descending by half-steps to as low as possible while remaining comfortably in head registration (light vocal mechanism).

Head Registration Isolation Through Variation of Dynamics and Vowels

Purpose 5-7

This exercise encourages a dynamic negotiation between the intrinsic laryngeal muscles—primarily the CT and TA—by using a variety of vowels and volumes. Even while maintaining head registration, there are adjustments in the mechanics of the voice that involve passive and active engagement for pitch, volume, and vowel changes. The male singer will find more control and flexibility throughout their range and better management in the secondo passaggio as a result of Exercise 5–7.

Figure 5-7. Notation for "Head Registration Isolation Through Variation of Dynamics and Vowels."

Exercise 5-7

Begin on /u/ at a starting pitch of C5 (or G4 as necessary) and sing a five-note descending scale; move to an /o/, /a/, or /i/ changing the dynamic to mezzo forte (mf) and sing a three-note ascending scale while still maintaining the head registration at a louder dynamic (Figure 5–7). Descend by half-steps and repeat the exercise to a comfortable low range. The volume of the first phase of the exercise is extremely soft with a clear, resonant head registration. At a lower pitch range, males may naturally adjust to a chest registration in a light vocal mechanism.

Primo and Secondo Passaggio

The word *passaggio* is an Italian term that means passage. In singing, the term is associated with historical Western classical voice pedagogy. It is used to identify the transition between the vocal registers often called *head voice* (registration) and *chest voice* (registration). The transition area is sometimes called a "break" because the voice may require a laryngeal mode or acoustic adjustment in order to not "break" or "crack." A goal of classical voice training is a seamless passaggio/register transition so that a unified vocal timbre is maintained. In CCM, often times a deliberate aesthetic change in timbre is preferred as a result of the passaggio. Considerations regarding the passaggio must take into account both laryngeal source and acoustic adjustments. As in other voice topics, there is disagreement about exactly where the exact transition pitches occur for each voice type.

Building a Bridge Across Registers

Purpose 5–8

Singing effortlessly through the secondo passaggio is an important aspect of training the male voice. It requires a dynamic interplay between the intrinsic laryngeal muscles, reduced transglottal air pressure, and skillful management of the resonance strategy. Exercise 5–8 is designed to focus on the skillful transition between the TA and CT muscles, air pressure, and airflow adjustments necessary for passaggio events.

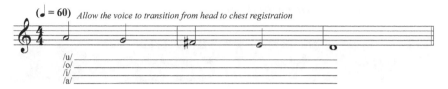

Figure 5–8. Notation for "Building a Bridge Across Registers."

 Exercise 5–8

Begin in head registration somewhere between A4 and C5 depending on the individual needs of the singer. Descend slowly on a five-note scale singing /u/ (Figure 5–8). Allow the voice to seamlessly transition to the chest registration on the pitch where it is naturally inclined to do so. This will vary depending on voice type. Descend by half-steps and repeat the exercise until all notes remain in chest registration. The volume will vary depending on the skill of the singer during the area of transition, but eventually should be practiced in a variety of dynamic ranges. The register transition should be as smooth as possible. This skill may take time to develop. After mastering /u/, practice the exercise on /o/, /a/, or /i/ to explore the changes required to navigate registration events on different vowels. Singers will need to moderate breath pressure so as not to hyperfunction when transitioning to chest registration. Make certain there is no laryngeal recruitment (an engagement resulting in a negative consequence), which will be evident by an elevated larynx and/or a strained vocal quality. Sometimes gently placing a pointer finger and thumb on either side of the thyroid cartilage (front of larynx) stabilizes the larynx inclined to elevate during the transition. Alternatively, place a thumb and finger on the thyrohyoid gap (Figure 4–5B) (space between the thyroid cartilage and hyoid bone) to monitor laryngeal elevation.

Male Registration Coordination

Head Registration to Develop High Notes in Chest Registration

Purpose 5–9

Expanding the upper range in chest registration is a primary goal of any male singer in both classical and CCM genres. Maintaining the chest voice across the secondo passaggio requires skillful resonance strategy and management of the breath so as not to cause hyperfunction of air pressure (Exercise 5–9). A principal goal is to release any recruitment in extrinsic or intrinsic laryngeal muscles to stabilize the larynx as they often want to provide assistance during this transition. Initiating voice production in head registration allows the CT muscle to be more active with a more passive TA muscle before transitioning to chest registration when the TA muscle is activated. This enables better negotiation between the two antagonist muscles, which can help enable efficient high notes. Finding the correct vocal tract shape will optimize resonance strategy crucial for stability.

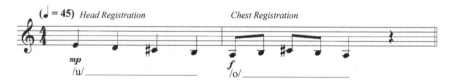

Figure 5–9. Notation for "Head Registration to Develop High Notes in Chest Registration."

 Exercise 5–9

Sing a descending five-note scale on /u/ in the lightest (soft) head registration. When arriving at the lowest note, transition to chest registration on an /o/ at a forte (f) dynamic on a three-note ascending/descending scale (Figure 5–9). Ascend by half-steps and repeat the exercise until the top chest registration note is sung without any recruitment. The starting note will vary greatly between singers but most likely will be between D4 and G4. Most important is that the starting note should be in the lightest vocal mechanism (regardless of registration) so that the singer can begin the 2nd phase of the exercise in chest registration at a comfortable pitch. This will be determined by the ability to efficiently switch to chest registration and continue the ascending scale. At the note of transition to chest registration, be certain that there is no forward jaw protrusion, laryngeal elevation, or tongue depression and that the breath does not hyperfunction, as these are common undesirable patterns of recruitment. They give the singer a feeling of perceived control but do not produce efficient singing. It is best to sequence head registration isolation vocal exercises previous to Exercise 5–9 for better coordination of high notes.

Messa di Voce Through the Secondo Passaggio

Purpose 5–10

Messa di voce exercises emanate from Western classical pedagogical literature dating back to the 18th and 19th centuries. For sound quality to remain constant, the exercise requires an extreme level of vocal coordination of the gradual abductory/adductory vocal fold gesture and breath pressure changes during the dynamic range (Titze & Verdolini-Abbott, 2012). The motor skill acquisition of learning to balance these two components (laryngeal muscle activity and breath pressure changes) is crucial to a singer's technique. Messa di voce should be sung throughout the vocal range but in this particular exercise, is designed for the male singer to negotiate registration transitions (Exercise 5–10).

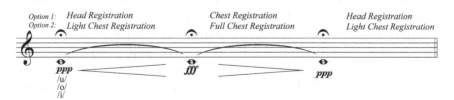

Figure 5–10. Notation for "Messa di Voce Through the Secondo Passaggio."

Exercise 5–10

Option 1: Choose a note that is comfortable in both chest and head registration (around C4). Sustain a single pitch on an /u/ and gradually crescendo/decrescendo across 5 s to 10 s (Figure 5–10). The tessitura will vary greatly by voice type, age, and skill level but is intended to be in the range of A3–G4. Not every singer will sing every note in that range. Each phase (crescendo/decrescendo) of this exercise should be even in time. Allow the voice to seamlessly transition from head to chest registration and back to head during the crescendo/decrescendo. This may take time to develop. Repeat the exercise on different pitches and on different vowels. At the transition note to chest registration, make certain the jaw does not protrude forward, the larynx does not elevate, the tongue does not depress, and the breath is not hyperfunctioning as these are common patterns of muscle recruitment that give the singer a feeling of perceived control. Option 2: A second version of this exercise is to maintain chest registration throughout the exercise on a continuum from light to full chest vocal mechanism (instead of transitioning from head registration to chest registration) and back on the crescendo/decrescendo for complete voice training.

Female Chest Registration Isolation

Chest Registration Isolation

Purpose 5–11 A and B

Registration isolation has become an accepted tradition for training singers of all genres. The following chest registration dominant exercises (Exercise 5–11 A and B) may be foreign to some female singers, especially those solely classically trained, but are necessary for a balanced singing voice. For those who sing predominantly in head registration and are unfamiliar with chest voice production, these exercises will lead to better vocal fold closure and clearer sound quality. Cross-training develops the voice so that one can access of variety of aesthetic possibilities. The degree of brassy resonance will depend on the singer's experience with this voice production. Volume is achieved through a dynamic balance between intrinsic laryngeal muscle coordination and resonance strategy. The brighter the /æ/, the brassier the timbre. The ascending/descending pattern in Exercise 5–11B is to help coordinate the intrinsic laryngeal muscle negotiation and air pressure changes discussed in the previous chapter as the pitch moves gradually higher in range.

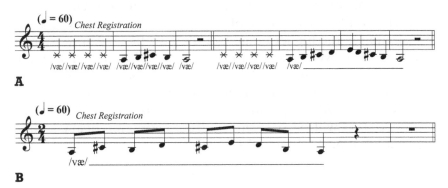

Figure 5–11. A–B. Notation for "Chest Registration Isolation."

Exercise 5–11 A and B

Begin the exercise by speaking /væ/ at a comfortable, resonant speaking pitch in rhythm, then proceed directly to either notation (Figure 5–11A or B). The first sung pitch should be /A3/ for females (lower or higher as appropriate) and C3 for males. Some singers new to chest registration and/or a brassy resonance strategy may need to stay within an interval of a 3rd before proceeding to a 5th (Figure 5–11A). For singers unfamiliar with this aesthetic, it can be beneficial to speak /væ/ prior to singing. This can help bridge the voice production between speaking and singing in chest voice. Until one can speak /væ/ with brassy, forward resonance, do not proceed. Be certain to use a megaphone vocal tract shape. Ascend by half-steps and repeat the exercise of choice, moving toward the highest chest register pitch that is comfortable; this may be as low as G4 (females) for someone new to belting or as high as E5 for a more experienced CCM singer. The /v/ provides benefits of a semi-occlusion to encourage a stable larynx and therefore it may be beneficial to repeat the /væ/ syllable on each pitch.

Head Registration to Facilitate
Efficient Chest Registration

Purpose 5–12

This exercise encourages a lighter chest registration by first initiating vocal production in head registration in the female voice (Exercise 5–12). This will enable a singer to maintain a chest-mix registration in the higher range by training a flexible and dynamic antagonism between the TA and CT muscles. The presumption is that by first activating the CT muscle for light head registration previous to shifting to chest registration (TA activation), the voice negotiates a more balanced vocal production in a brassy, chest aesthetic. This will prevent singers from taking too heavy a chest registration (vocal fold mass) to a higher tessitura.

Figure 5–12. Notation for "Head Registration to Facilitate Efficient Chest Registration."

Exercise 5–12

Sing a five-note descending scale on a soft, resonant /u/ in head registration until the bottom note, then transition to chest registration on an /æ/ three-note ascending scale at a louder volume (Figure 5–12). The starting pitch will begin in the range of E4–G4. The first phase of the exercise may require singers to be in either a light chest or head registration, depending on the pitch; the ideal is a CT-dominant voice production, but either is sufficient to experience the benefits. Repeat the exercise, ascending by half-steps until the top note of a comfortable chest voice. Use both audible and visual cues to observe any recruitment or strain in the sound as the chest registration ascends in pitch and volume. Over time, singers will find it easier to sing chest registration higher in a variety of volumes. For many, it is easier to sing chest registration in a higher range at louder volumes than a lighter chest-mix production in a higher range. Training the intrinsic laryngeal muscles to negotiate a variety of volumes and vowels in different ratios of perceived registration takes time. The goal is to sing at any dynamic level, piano to forte, in a chest voice production at a higher chest registration tessitura (A4–F5).

The Belt Aesthetic

As a precursor to exercises focused on a belt aesthetic, it is helpful to begin with sounds, words, or phrases that holistically produce emotional triggers when calling or yelling. In the book *Cross-Training in the Voice Studio*, Spivey and Saunders-Barton use many phrases to naturally excite the correct voice production for belting. In particular, the phrase "hey taxi" is very useful in teaching the coordination necessary for a loud dynamic with a great deal of brassy resonance. The expression "hey taxi" emanates from circumstances one can relate to, needing to loudly get the attention of a taxi driver, and naturally facilitates a brassy sound. Another scenario is to imagine calling a dog as if it were about to be hit by a car. Our body and voice naturally make the necessary adjustments to capture the dog or driver's attention under such dangerous circumstances. A common dog name that is useful is Max. The /m/ and /æ/ encourage a brassy resonance to facilitate the acoustic energy necessary for high intensity belt sounds. Practice calling "hey, taxi" or "hey, Max" while imagining those situations until brassy resonant sensations are experienced prior to singing belt exercises.

Building a Bridge to Belting

Purpose 5–13 A–C

Since most females in modern times (postfeminism) speak in chest registration, using words and expressions that facilitate speech-like vocal production encourage a healthy belt aesthetic (assuming the singer's speaking voice is well produced). Exercise 5–13A was inspired by a workshop at the NATS National Convention in 2018 with Norman Spivey and Mary Saunders Barton. Similar exercises can be found in *Cross-Training in the Voice Studio* (Spivey & Saunders-Barton, 2018).

A

Figure 5–13. A–C. Notation for "Building a Bridge to Belting." *continues*

Exercise 5–13 A

Speak the phrase "may I go" with a brassy resonance. Linger on the /m/ before moving to the vowel to encourage the kinesthetic feeling of forward sensations. As shown in Figure 5–13, sing scale degrees 1-5-1 on the words "may I go." Begin around an A4 (females) and C3 (males). The range varies but ascends to a top note around C5/D5 (females) and C4/D4 (males), eventually belting as high as F5 for advanced female belters and above an F4 for the male singer. Classically trained singers may be inclined to add lofted resonance (lengthened vocal tract, tall vowels) to certain words, but this will not facilitate the belt aesthetic. Lean toward an /æ/ instead of an /a/ on the word "I" and a closed /o/ on the word "go." It is useful to place the semi-glide /j/ of "may" on the higher pitch with the word "I." The gesture of /j/ is useful in preventing singers from gripping or bracing with the tongue. Advance to the octave "may I go" after the fifth interval becomes efficient.

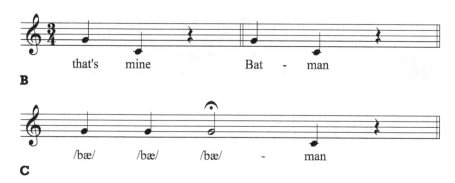

B

C

Figure 5–13. *continued*

Exercise 5–13 B and C

Use the phrase "that's mine" and sing the notation shown in Figure 5–13B with a starting pitch around G4 (females) and G3 (males). The tongue must remain liquid when forming the /ð/ onset of the word "that." The /ð/ is a semi-occluded gesture used prior to the "brassy" /æ/ to discourage the larynx from elevating. It is important to not inadvertently recruit or brace with the tongue when initiating a vocal onset with a dental consonant before a belt aesthetic. If a singer exhibits articulatory tongue challenges, substitute the word "batman" to take advantage of the plosive bilabial /b/ instead. Figure 5–13C is used to develop a sustained belt on high notes, which requires specific endurance training of extrinsic and intrinsic laryngeal muscles. Sing the syllable /ba/ and hold it for 3 to 5 s (or longer) before returning to the bottom note. This exercise promotes an efficient belt aesthetic to C5 (beginners) and F5 or above (advanced) for females and F4 and above for the male voice. Although there are no "magic exercises" for teaching singing, when it comes to coordinating a belt vocal production, this task comes close. It is extremely useful for introducing belt sounds or training the extended range necessary for high intensity chest registration.

Mixed Registration for a Broad Spectrum of Sound

"Meow" CCM Mixed Registration

Purpose 5-14

Learning to make intrinsic laryngeal muscle adjustments along with resonance strategy choices for the production of a multitude of sounds is an important aspect of a CCM singers training. Most of the time (not always), one can ascertain if a singer is in a more head or chest registration dominant vocal production. Exercise 5-14 is used to condition chest registration and head registration in such a way that a singer arrives at a blended mixed registration CCM aesthetic across a broad pitch range.

Figure 5-14. Notation for "'Meow' CCM Mixed Registration."

Exercise 5-14

Sing "meow" on a five-note ascending/descending scale with a starting pitch around A3 (females) and F3 (males) (Figure 5-14). Ascend by half-steps, making certain transitions through registration events are seamless; it will require a lighter chest registration for this to be achieved. The combination of sounds on the word "meow" facilitates a nice mixed register and resonance strategy. There should be very little perceptual change in sound quality throughout the exercise.

"My"—CCM Mixed Registration

Purpose 5-15

The combination of sounds on the syllable "my" are helpful for developing mixed registration. The /m/ encourages forward resonant sensations and the diphthong requires a flexible tongue. Exercise 5–15 crosses an octave range in an arpeggio to develop light, seamless transitions across the registers. This discourages a pressed sound when coordinating a seamless transition between chest and head registration and requires a light vocal mechanism so that adjustments between the TA and CT muscles, air pressure and flow, and resonance strategies are efficient.

Figure 5–15. Notation for "'My'—CCM Mixed Registration."

Exercise 5–15

Sing "my" on the arpeggio as shown in Figure 5–15 beginning around C4 (females) and C3 (males). Ascend by half-steps and repeat the exercise, allowing the voice to seamlessly and naturally move through registration transitions so that the quality of the sound has little perceptual difference. Female singers may need to begin on a lower note, such as A3, to settle into a light chest registration before the transition note to head registration occurs. There should be no sensation of pressure or strain in the larynx. Continue to a comfortable high note.

Arpeggio Mixed Registration

Purpose 5–16

The ability to quickly and seamlessly transition from chest to head registration is important for singers. The importance of the negotiation of the intrinsic laryngeal muscles and their relationship to air pressure and airflow along with resonance strategies cannot be underestimated. Exercise 5–16 incorporates /ja/ during the octave interval to condition flexibility within the articulatory system. Developing independence between the interconnections of the articulation system is an integral part of voice training and is further explored in Chapter 6.

Figure 5–16. Notation for "Arpeggio Mixed Registration."

Exercise 5–16

With a starting pitch around C5 (females) and C4 (males), sing an /i/ triplet descending arpeggio (8-5-3-1) switching to /ja/ ("ya") on the bottom note to an octave jump (1-8-1) (Figure 5–16). Be certain to use only the tongue and not the jaw during the articulation of the /ja/. The tongue should flex easily toward the roof of the mouth for the gesture of /ja/. Do not tense or brace with the tongue dorsum on /ja/, especially in a higher tessitura. Ascend by half-steps, allowing the voice to seamlessly blend through registration transitions to the highest comfortable note. Registration choices will be gender and singer dependent. A male singer may be able to remain in chest registration quite high in a broad spectrum of CCM sound productions or may move back and forth between registers as seamlessly as possible. A female will inevitably move back and forth between registers until a high tessitura is reached, at which point she will then remain in head registration. The approach will require resonance strategy adjustments through vocal tract shaping to accommodate the desired sound. The vowels /i/ and /a/ are adjusted accordingly, either bright with a divergent vocal tract (megaphone) shape or warm with a convergent vocal tract (inverted megaphone) shape depending on whether a brassy or more lofted resonant timbre is desired. There should be very little perceptual sound quality change within this exercise.

Ode to Joan Lader

Purpose 5–17

The purpose of exercise 5–17 is to coordinate many aspects of vocal function in one challenging task. This includes balanced staccato vocal onsets and offsets followed directly by a legato phrase across a broad pitch range. (Refer to Chapter 4, the phonation chapter, for a detailed discussion on singing staccato.) Moving from staccato to legato in quick succession requires significant coordination of respiration, phonation, registration, and resonance. The resonance strategy of this exercise could be altered for a broad spectrum of CCM or classical sound production, depending on the needs of the singer. This exercise was inspired by Joan Lader's *Working in the Theatre: Vocal Coach* (2018).

Figure 5–17. Notation for "Ode to Joan Lader."

Exercise 5–17

Sing a light staccato /a/ on each note, followed by legato on the second phase of the exercise (Figure 5–17). As previously discussed, balanced onsets on vowel-initiated syllables may require the intent of a silent /h/ to facilitate efficient singing. The starting pitch will be around A3/C4 (females) and C3 (males). Ascend by half-steps and repeat the exercise to a comfortable high note. This exercise has a multitude of possibilities for registration, including timbral choices, and will be gender and singer dependent. A male singer may be able to remain in chest registration quite high or may move back and forth between registers as smoothly as possible. A female will inevitably move back and forth between registers until a high tessitura is reached, at which point she will remain in head registration. The approach will require resonance strategy adjustments to accommodate the desired sound on a continuum between bright or warm /a/. There should be very little perceptual sound quality change within the exercise, regardless of genre.

Alternating Registration

Purpose 5–18

The ability to quickly switch from head registration to chest registration in one exercise is excellent for cross-training purposes.

Female singers will kinesthetically experience the physiological and acoustic differences between the two registers in quick succession in Exercise 5–18. The main intent of this exercise is for the female voice to directly alternate registration changes (laryngeal source and acoustic adjustments) on the same series of pitches in the middle range. The ability to skillfully do so demonstrates technical control. Previous exercises in this chapter focused on the male voice, deliberately alternating laryngeal source transitions, and in this exercise, males will explore resonant strategy adjustments in quick succession through vocal tract shaping, not laryngeal source changes.

Figure 5–18. Notation for "Alternating Registration."

Exercise 5–18

Begin in head registration (females) with lofted resonance singing /mi/-/me/-/ma/-/mo/-/mu/; take a breath and repeat the same pattern (/mi/-/me/-/ma/-/mo/-/mu/) in chest registration with brassy resonance (Figure 5–18). Female voices will experience more extreme differences in timbre and sensations of voice production as they make both laryngeal source and acoustic adjustments. This exercise is practiced between C4 as the bottom note and C5/D5 as the top note (female), depending on the training of the singer. Males will sing an octave lower. Singers may or may not stay entirely in the perceived head and chest registration as listed, depending on individual needs. Perhaps a singer will stay in a head registration on the lowest notes, even though the sound will be weaker, to strengthen that mode of voice production. Ascend/descend by half-steps and repeat the exercise in the middle of the vocal range. Be certain that the jaw does not move when the pitch moves. When the vowel stays the same, there is no need for the jaw to move on a major third interval. The jaw should only move to make the /m/ and even then mitigated as much as possible.

Mastering Messa di Voce

Purpose 5–19

Exercise 5–19 was previously discussed in Exercise 5–10 under "Male Registration Coordination." Messa di voce is listed in this section to include the female voice. The exercise involves a controlled crescendo/decrescendo (Figure 5–19). For sound quality to remain constant, this exercise requires the ultimate control of the gradual abductor/adductor vocal fold gesture and lung pressure changes during the dynamic range (Titze & Verdolini-Abbott, 2012). The motor skill acquisition of learning to balance these two components (laryngeal muscle activity and lung pressure changes) is important in singing technique. During the crescendo and decrescendo of this exercise there is a challenging negotiation of the intrinsic laryngeal muscles on a continuum of activity as well as breath pressure changes that help in the dynamic negotiation of vocal function. Historically, messa di voce was used for training classical singers; for males, this would have been chest registration and for females, it would have been head registration.

Figure 5–19. Notation for "Mastering Messa di Voce."

Exercise 5–19

Choose any vowel (/a/, /e/, /i/, /o/, /u/) and sing a single pitch on a crescendo/decrescendo across 5 s to 10 s (Figure 5–19). Each phase of the exercise (crescendo/decrescendo) should be even in time. Repeat the exercise to practice each pitch within an octave C3 to C4 (males) and C4 to C5 (females). Alternate vowels and notice the impact on the voice systems. There will be considerations of breath management and resonance strategy alterations. The vowels are adjusted accordingly, either bright with a divergent vocal tract (megaphone) shape or warm with a convergent vocal tract (inverted megaphone) shape depending on whether a brassier or more lofted resonant timbre is preferred. Broadly speaking, females will transition to head registration around E4, although one could choose to use the exercise to develop a chest-dominant registration, depending on an individual's needs. The male singer will remain in chest registration for this exercise.

Summary

Discussions around registration are challenging to navigate. There are many divergent theories about registers, some based on scientific evidence while others are more subjective. Manuel Garcia was one of the first to provide a scientific definition of registers in the 19th century, and the debates among voice pedagogues have only intensified since that time. There is still much to be learned about laryngeal source adjustments and acoustic interactions within a particular series of pitches. Research is ongoing and will continue to inform voice teachers of fact-based information. An ongoing understanding between science-based research and practice-based research is crucial when approaching discussions on registration. The sensory experience of registration events is very individual and multifaceted across gender, genre, voice type, and training. Semantics aside, voice teachers must find a way to train balanced registration regardless of debates about terminology. Each teacher must find science-informed strategies to enable a language that works in the context of studio application. This may include terms influenced by sensations from which to create a dialogue for building a functional singing technique.

References

Bozeman, K. (2013). *Practical vocal acoustics: Pedagogic applications for teachers and singers.* Hillsdale, NY: Pendragon Press.

Coffin, B. (1987). *Coffin's sounds of singing: Principles and applications of vocal techniques with chromatic vowel chart* (2nd ed.). Metuchen, NJ: The Scarecrow Press.

Hoch, M., & Sandage, M. J. (2017). Working toward a common vocabulary: Reconciling the terminology of teachers of singing, voice scientists, and speech-language pathologists. *Journal of Voice, 31*(6), 647–648.

Kochis-Jennings, K. S., Finnegan, E. M., Hoffman, H. T., Jaiswal, S., & Hull, D. (2014). Cricothyroid muscle and thyroarytenoid muscle dominance in vocal register control: Preliminary results. *Journal of Voice, 28*(5), 652.

Lader, J. (2018). *Working in the theatre: Vocal coach* [Video file]. Retrieved from https://www.youtube.com/watch?v=HQgJTE1qI8w&feature=you tu.be&fbclid=IwAR3CAlor1mIDSBEJbx17fDG8yNqHKYI1_ni4ydOOhh LZLIrpUe6MStZ-tbQ

LeBorgne, W. D., & Rosenberg, M. (2014). *The vocal athlete.* San Diego, CA: Plural Publishing.

LoVetri, J. (2008). Contemporary commercial music. *Journal of Voice, 22*(3), 260–262.

McCoy, S. (2012). *Your voice: An inside view* (2nd ed.) Delaware, OH: Inside View Press.

McCoy, S. (2019). *Your voice: An inside view* (3rd ed.), Delaware, OH: Inside View Press.

Reid, C. (1972). *The free voice.* New York, NY: The Joseph Patelson Music House.

Reid, C. (1990). *Bel Canto: Principles and practices.* New York, NY: Joseph Patelson Music House. (Original work published 1950)

Roubeau, B., Henrich, N., & Castellengo, M. (2009). Laryngeal vibratory mechanisms: The notion of vocal register revisited. *Journal of Voice, 23*(4), 425–438.

Spivey, N., & Saunders-Barton, M. (2018). *Cross-training in the voice studio: A balancing act.* San Diego, CA: Plural Publishing.

Titze, I. (2000). *Principles of voice production.* Iowa City, IA: National Center for Voice and Speech.

Titze, I., & Verdolini-Abbott, K. V. (2012). *Vocology: The science and practice of voice habilitation.* Salt Lake City, UT: National Center for Voice and Speech.

Titze, I. R. (2018). Mixed registration. *Journal of Singing, 75*(1), 49–50.

Selected Resources

Abitbol, J. (2019). *The female voice.* San Diego, CA: Plural Publishing.

The Academy of American Voice Teachers. (2014). *In support of contemporary commercial music (nonclassical) voice pedagogy.* Retrieved from http://www.americanacademyofteachersofsinging.org/assets/articles/ CCMVoicePedagogy.pdf

Bozeman, K. (2010). The role of the first formant in training the male singing voice. *Journal of Singing, 66*(3), 291–297.

Bozeman, K. (2013). Acoustic passaggio pedagogy for the male voice. *Logopedics Phoniatrics Vocology, 38*(2), 64-69.

Brunssen, K. (2018). *The evolving singing voice: Changes across the lifespan.* San Diego, CA: Plural Publishing.

Cooksey, J. M. (1999). *Working with adolescent voices.* St. Louis, MO: Concordia Publishing House.

Herbst, C. T., & Švec, J. G. (2014). Adjustments of glottal configuration in singing. *Journal of Singing, 70*(3), 301–308.

Jackson Hearns, L., & Kremer, B. (2018). *The singing teacher's guide to transgender voices.* San Diego, CA: Plural Publishing.

Kochis-Jennings, K. S., Finnegan, E. M., Hoffman, H. T., & Jaiswal, S. (2012). Laryngeal muscle activity and vocal fold adduction during chest, chestmix, headmix, and head registers in females. *Journal of Voice, 26*(2), 182–193.

Lessley, E. (2017). *Teaching transgender singers.* Seattle, WA: University of Washington.

Miller, R. (1986). *The structure of singing.* New York, NY: Schirmer.

Nix, J. (2018). The hole in the sky. *Journal of Singing, 74*(3), 273–278.

Phillips, K. H. (2014). *Teaching kids to sing* (2nd ed.). Independence, KY: Cengage.

Stemple, J. (1984). *Clinical voice pathology: Theory and management.* Columbus, OH: Merrill.

Titze, I. (2014). Bi-stable vocal fold adduction: A mechanism of modal-falsetto register shifts and mixed registration. *Journal of the Acoustical Society of America, 135*(4), 2091–2101.

Williams, J. (2018). *Teaching singing to children and young adults* (2nd ed.). Devon, UK: Compton.

Chapter 6

A Systematic Approach to Articulation

Articulation is the process by which the joint product of the vibrator and the resonators is shaped into recognizable speech sounds through the muscular adjustments and movements of the speech organs.

—James C. McKinney, *The Diagnosis & Correction of Vocal Faults* (1994), p. 27

Overview of Articulation

The structures of articulation include the jaw, tongue, palate, and pharynx. Interconnecting relationships between these muscle groups are complex. Many of the same structures used for articulation are involved in the biological functions of swallowing, chewing, and airway protection. Voice teachers must consider the biological aspects of the articulation system to understand circumstances in which a singer may work against the body's natural articulatory reflexes. For example, muscles involved in swallowing such as the digastric and mylohyoid both lower the jaw, which is necessary for singing, and elevate the larynx, which may be problematic if there is unwanted tension within that dynamic. As part of the process of directing food toward the esophagus during swallowing, the soft palate rises to close off the nasal passages and the larynx elevates to protect the airway. Singers must learn to overcome this natural tandem reflex of the soft palate and laryngeal elevation in order to find independent movement between these two structures. Voice teachers must gain knowledge of the complex nature of the articulation system to understand the implications for voice studio application (see the text box "Neutral Larynx" later in this chapter).

Muscles within the articulatory system also contribute to vocal tract shaping and, therefore, the acoustic landscape. The articulatory muscles are a primary component of resonance strategy and vocal timbre. Learning to shape the vocal tract in a way that does not negatively impact vocal function is an integral part of a singing technique. The acoustic implications are explored in Chapter 7.

The Jaw

The muscles of the jaw (mandible) activate to both open (depress) and close (elevate) the structure. Because the jaw elevator muscles are biologically stronger than the jaw depressor muscles for the purpose of chewing, this can present a challenge for singers. Singers must learn to sing with an open jaw position without letting the antagonistic jaw depressor and elevator muscles create unwanted tension. The primary jaw elevator muscles responsible for chewing are the masseter, internal (medial) pterygoid, and the temporalis (Figure 6–1). The muscle fibers of the masseter and its internal counterpart, the internal pterygoid, run diagonally from the cheekbone to below the jawline. The temporalis is a large muscle that covers most of the side of the head, and when contracted, is responsible for biting. Opening the jaw beyond what gravity offers is primarily the responsibility of the jaw depressor muscles (digastric, mylohyoid, geniohyoid; see Figure 6–1). These three dual-purpose muscles both open the jaw and elevate the larynx.

Although singers require antagonism for breath mechanics, a discussion of muscles of articulation demonstrates why it is not ideal within this system. If the muscles responsible for closing the jaw are tense, then the muscles that open the jaw may induce their secondary action, which is laryngeal elevation. This action is

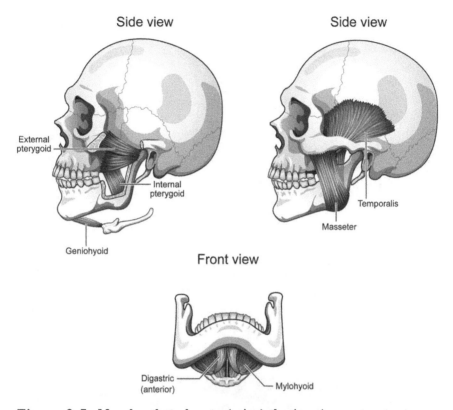

Figure 6–I. Muscles that elevate (raise) the jaw (masseter, temporalis, internal pterygoid) and depress (lower) the jaw (mylohyoid, geniohyoid, digastric [anterior], and external pterygoid). From *Foundations of Speech and Hearing* (p. 167), by J. D. Hoit and G. Weismer, 2018, San Diego: Plural Publishing. Copyright 2018 by Plural Publishing. Used with permission.

somewhat overcome by using muscles to anchor the larynx (sternohyoid, sternothyroid, and omohyoid; Figure 6–II), but a tug-of-war may result, impairing vocal freedom and efficiency (McCoy, 2012, p. 163). Taking time to stretch the muscles of the jaw will contribute to independence within the articulatory system and eliminate potential problems. Another important element of the jaw position is its impact on the shape of the vocal tract, which is a significant aspect of resonance strategy.

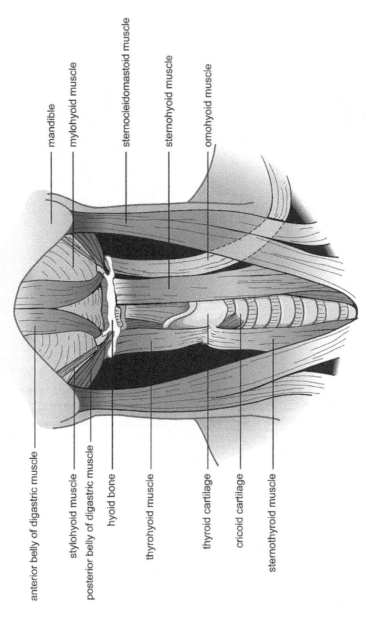

Figure 6–11. Extrinsic laryngeal muscles. From *Clinical Voice Pathology: Theory and Management* (6th ed., p. 31), by J. C. Stemple, N. Roy, and B. K. Klaben, 2020, San Diego, CA: Plural Publishing. Copyright 2020 by Plural Publishing. Used with permission.

anterior belly of digastric muscle

stylohyoid muscle

posterior belly of digastric muscle

hyoid bone

thyrohyoid muscle

thyroid cartilage

cricoid cartilage

sternothyroid muscle

mandible

mylohyoid muscle

sternocleidomastoid muscle

sternohyoid muscle

omohyoid muscle

The Tongue

Muscles of the tongue are both intrinsic (muscles within the tongue blade) and extrinsic (muscles of the tongue blade connected to elsewhere in the head or neck). The overall function of the four paired intrinsic tongue muscles (inferior and superior longitudinal, vertical, and transverse) is to shape the tongue. They lengthen, shorten, curl, uncurl, narrow, flatten, and widen the tongue as well as turn it upward and downward. The extrinsic tongue muscles (palatoglossus, genioglossus, styloglossus, and hyoglossus; Figure 6–III) are interconnected with either the palate, pharynx, jaw, or hyoid bone. They are responsible for extending, elevating, retracting, depressing, and curling the tongue. The tongue is vital for chewing and swallowing food as well as for speech. The correct position and shape of the tongue is critical for many aspects of singing, including the articulation of language and optimizing of vocal tract resonances. Due to the biological interconnections of the tongue necessary for

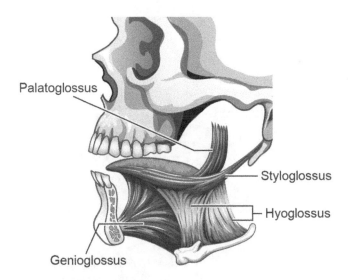

Figure 6–III. Extrinsic muscles of the tongue. These are the styloglossus, palatoglossus, hyoglossus, and genioglossus. Modified from *Foundations of Speech and Hearing* (p. 171), by J. D. Hoit and G. Weismer, 2018, San Diego, CA: Plural Publishing. Copyright 2018 by Plural Publishing. Used with permission.

activities such as swallowing, it is vital to train as much independent mobility as possible within its movement for efficient singing.

The Soft Palate

The soft palate (velum; Figure 6–IV) is part of the swallowing mechanism and moves in conjunction with the tongue, pharyngeal wall, and larynx. It participates in activities such as yawning, laughing, and sobbing. The soft palate is a complex series of muscles that retract and elevate to close the nasopharynx during swallowing and ensure that food and liquids are directed toward the esophagus and not into the nose. In speech and singing, this activation is necessary to separate the oral cavity from the nasal cavity to produce a more pleasant oral sound. Otherwise, air escapes through the nose and causes a nasal sound. However, some sounds like humming

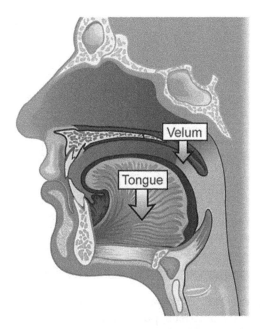

Figure 6–IV. Side view of the soft palate (velum) and tongue. From *Foundations of Speech and Hearing* (p. 147), by J. D. Hoit and G. Weismer, 2018, San Diego, CA: Plural Publishing. Copyright 2018 by Plural Publishing. Used with permission.

require the soft palate to be in a lower position to allow air to flow through the nasal cavity.

There is a great deal of discussion as to whether to deliberately teach active elevation of the soft palate in singing. Some voice teachers advocate allowing the movement to naturally occur without deliberate cueing, while others incorporate specific exercises as part of the training regime to cue soft palate elevation. Since the soft palate contributes to vocal timbre, awareness of the muscles that control the movement seems useful in voice training. It is certainly necessary to address the position of the soft palate when a singer is hypernasal. In singing, the soft palate impacts aesthetic choices that reside on a continuum from personal preference to genre specific expectations.

The Pharynx

The pharynx, commonly called the throat, is divided into three areas: the oropharynx, nasopharynx, and laryngopharynx (Figure 6–V).

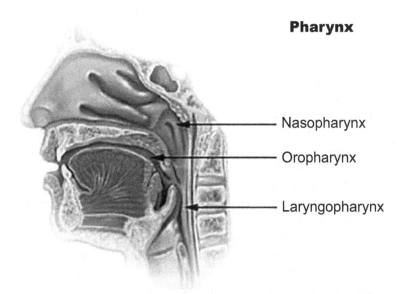

Pharynx

Nasopharynx

Oropharynx

Laryngopharynx

Figure 6–V. Lateral view of the pharynx. Adapted from *The Vocal Athlete* (p. 89), by W. D. LeBorgne and M. D. Rosenberg, 2014, San Diego, CA: Plural Publishing. *Courtesy of Wikimedia Commons.*

The pharynx serves both respiratory and digestive functions. Besides its biological necessity, it is a primary resonating chamber of the voice. It has a critical role in singing as it serves the purpose of selectively amplifying, to varying degrees of intensity, the sound waves produced by the vibrating vocal folds. When the pharynx changes shape, it is due to the engagement of the superior, inferior, and middle constrictor muscles. These muscles contribute to swallowing by narrowing the pharynx to direct food into the esophagus. Therefore, the pharynx is at its widest state when in a neutral position. Since the constrictor muscles are either tensed to narrow the pharynx or relaxed, this means there are no muscles that "open" the throat for singing. Singers often have a misconception about an "open throat," a commonly used expression amongst voice teachers. The kinesthetic mapping of the vocal tract shape, including the pharynx, must be carefully guided.

The Neutral Larynx

The biological function of the larynx requires it to have a flexible range. Finding the optimal vertical laryngeal position is an important part of a singer's training. It is determined by many factors, including genre. Depending on the aesthetic needs of a song, the optimal height of the larynx may be slightly higher or lower from its neutral position. Brassy resonance strategy used within the broad spectrum of CCM requires a shortened vocal tract; the larynx may be in a neutral-high position to achieve the appropriate sound quality. Lofted resonance used by Western classical singers employs a lengthened vocal tract; the larynx may be in a neutral-low position to achieve the appropriate resonance strategy. Functional singing does not advocate a depressed or elevated larynx that would negatively affect vocal production. In this text, the larynx position refers to neutral-high or neutral-low with the understanding that it resides on a continuum suitable for efficient singing and aesthetic outcomes.

Teacher Takeaways of Articulation

As voice athletes, it is essential for singers to acquire independence within the articulation system. Voice teachers must understand the potential impact of the interconnections between articulation and the other voice systems because there is potential for unwanted muscular antagonism and recruitment (engagement resulting in a negative consequence). Learning about the body's natural reflexes is useful for informing the design of vocal exercises. Practice sessions for singers should include tongue, jaw, and soft palate stretches to encourage independence between these structures. The goal is to increase awareness of their movement both independently and interdependently. Voice teachers are encouraged to find pedagogical resources to study (in detail) the interconnections between the articulatory muscles.

Application of Articulation

Designing vocal exercises to condition a maximum degree of independence between the various articulatory muscles is imperative for developing vocal efficiency and minimizing the potential for unwanted engagement. The following tasks encourage flexibility and independent mobility between the jaw, tongue, palate, and larynx, with the intent of developing a functional singing technique. Often, a byproduct of inadvertent muscle antagonism or recruitment is obvious while singing. Vocal challenges such as a shaking jaw or depressed tongue are easy to identify. At other times, inadvertent muscle antagonism must be intuited based on sound production, such as strain or stridency in the tone.

Singers are encouraged to embrace the process of releasing unwanted articulatory muscle engagement, which may be disorienting until a more comfortable and efficient singing technique emerges. The tongue and jaw provide a strong sense of perceived control that can lead to problematic vocal function. Singers sometimes inadvertently try to stabilize the larynx or to produce resonance by ineffective recruitment of the tongue. Since some of the articulators are movable and a primary contributor to resonance, it is easy to misinterpret their intended actions. As a singer relinquishes unwanted engagement within the articulation system, it facilitates a recalibration of the voice systems, since changing one part of the system affects the other parts and the whole. It is a remarkable kinesthetic transformation when a singer habilitates optimal breath management and resonance strategies in lieu of articulatory tension. Acquiring new patterns of vocal efficiency can be a frustrating process that needs to be embraced until singers realize they have other means of control. A great deal of patience, persistence, and enthusiastic support are required.

As discussed in Chapter 1, kinesthetic singing tools are effective to facilitate a change in voice production. This chapter introduces several, including gauze, candy, wine cork, straws, a mirror, and thumbs. Eventually, the kinesthetic singing tools will be used only as an infrequent reset. Because muscles of articulation have a profound impact on the other systems of the voice, exercises designed with an awareness of the numerous muscular intricacies are essential.

Jaw Stretches

Preparing the Jaw

Purpose 6–1 A to E

Muscles of the jaw are under pressure from chewing, talking, and other motions. Stretching the muscles of the jaw prior to singing encourages the release of unwanted tension and promotes independent mobility between antagonistic jaw depressor and elevator muscles. As part of their daily practice, singers should take time to include jaw stretches in their routine. The following five stretches initiate movement in a variety of directions (Exercise 6–1 A–E).

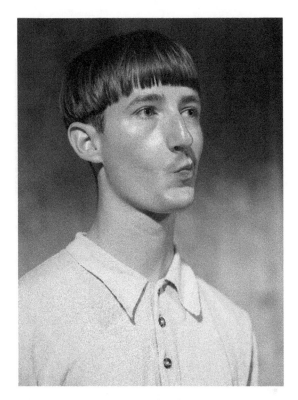

Figure 6–1A. Image of a singer demonstrating jaw movement in a circular motion.

 Exercise 6–1 A

Gently move the jaw in a circular clockwise motion. Use a small range of motion with the lips remaining closed. Slowly increase the range of motion, eventually allowing the lips to part as the jaw opens. Reverse the movement to a counterclockwise direction and repeat.

Exercise 6–1 B

Figure 6–1B. Image of a singer simulating chewing salt-water taffy for jaw mobility.

Imagine chewing salt-water taffy. Allow the jaw to gently and flexibly move in a chewing fashion that would be necessary for the chewy candy. Explore a variety of directions and range with the jaw movement. Add a humming pitch glide along with this stretch to layer an element of voicing onto the task.

Exercise 6–1 C

Figure 6–1C. Image of a singer demonstrating a jaw stretch with lip retraction.

Gently extend the jaw down and back while retracting your lips as far as is comfortable and hold the stretch for 5 to 10 s. Release the stretch and repeat the gesture a few times. Next, move in the opposite direction and bring the jaw forward with lips puckered and hold the stretch 5 to 10 s. Repeat the gesture a few times, being careful to move slowly and gently. The jaw should remain flexible, never locked or rigid.

Exercise 6–1 D

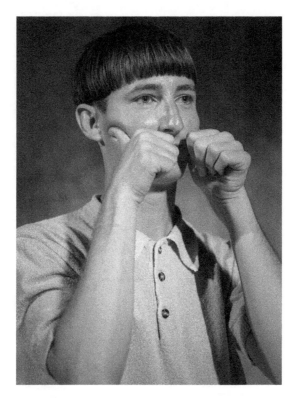

Figure 6–1D. Image of a singer demonstrating the position for a release of the masseter muscle.

Locate the top of the masseter muscle by placing each thumb on the underside of the cheekbone (zygomatic arch) in the notch. Be certain the correct area is located, then clench the jaw. A slight bulge outward will reveal the activation of the masseter muscle. The masseter is a primary muscle for chewing. It also engages when people grind their teeth at night, and, therefore, the area may be tender. All the more reason to include gentle massage in the daily routine. One can massage the masseter by either constant pressure or small kneading circles, as both are appropriate. Continue massaging while slowly extending to the point of maximum opening for a high note.

Exercise 6–1 E

Figure 6–1E. Image of a singer demonstrating the position for a release of the temporalis muscle release.

Place each hand on the side of the head in the area around the temples and clench. The muscle being flexed outward is the temporalis, which is used to elevate the jaw for biting. Place light pressure on the area and massage with the palm of the hands while slowly opening and closing the jaw to achieve a stretch. This is a good stretch to explore an open neutral resting jaw position, how much depression can be comfortably achieved, and the natural inclination for the direction of the jaw movement. Ideally, it will move freely down in a neutral position.

IPA Symbols Used in Chapter 6

/a/ as in br**igh**t (pre-diphthong)

/e/ as in **a**te (pre-dipthong)

/ɪ/ as in d**ig**

/i/ as in m**ee**t

/j/ as in **y**ap

/g/ as in **g**o

/k/ as in **k**itten

/l/ as in **l**ap

/d/ as in **d**og

/n/ as in **n**ap

/t/ as in **t**oy

Figure 6–VI. Image of a keyboard with pitch notation.

Jaw: Voiced Exercises

Wine Cork Between Front Teeth

Purpose 6–2

The wine cork is used to bring awareness to an open and stable jaw position while singing (see the text box "Wine Cork" later in this chapter). Exercise 6–2 uses the wine cork to encourage a release of unwanted tension between the antagonistic jaw elevator and depressor muscles. Singers may also become aware of clenching or displacing the jaw forward while using this kinesthetic tool.

Since muscles of the jaw insert into the larynx at the hyoid bone, unwanted jaw tension can have a profound impact on vocal function. The wine cork may further reduce unwanted engagement of the tongue due to the articulatory interconnections.

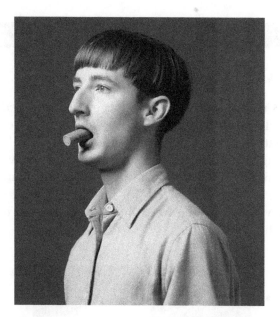

Figure 6–2. Image of singer demonstrating "Wine Cork Between Front Teeth."

Exercise 6–2

Place a wine cork between the front teeth as shown in Figure 6–2. The cork should be unobtrusive to the tongue position, which should lie naturally on the floor of the mouth underneath the cork. The teeth lightly hold the cork, but the jaw should feel disengaged from any unwanted engagement. Speak /a/ several times, making certain it sounds speechlike, natural, without inadvertent tongue engagement, and with forward resonance. Sing an ascending/descending five-note scale or octave in a comfortable range. Ascend by half-steps and repeat the chosen pattern several times. Remove the cork and continue singing. The jaw should feel a sense of release if there was previously unwanted engagement. The cork can be used while singing any vocal exercise or repertoire. Alternate a section of repertoire with and without the cork to condition the benefits of this kinesthetic tool. If the song ascends above F4 for men or G5 for women, it may be necessary to momentarily hold the cork with the fingers in order to appropriately open the jaw for a higher tessitura.

Wine Cork Between Molars

Purpose 6–3

Exercise 6–3 uses a wine cork to disengage unwanted tension of the jaw muscles, differently than the previous exercise. By placing an appropriately sized wine cork (see the text box "Wine Cork" on facing page) between the molars, a distinct jaw opening is achieved, which can be beneficial to a lofted resonance strategy. This exercise is particularly helpful for singers with stridency in the voice or voices needing to explore more warmth in the upper tessitura of their sound.

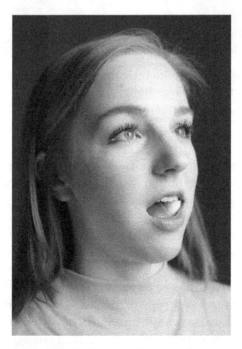

Figure 6–3. Image of singer demonstrating "Wine Cork Between Molars."

Exercise 6–3

Cut the wine cork in half (round side) and place the flat side in between the back molars (Figure 6–3). The wine cork should be cut at a height suitable for a comfortably open jaw position while singing: F/G4 (males) and F/G5 (females). The tongue should be in a neutral /a/ position underneath the cork resting on the floor of the mouth. The teeth will hold the cork in place (do not clench the teeth), and the jaw should feel disengaged. Speak /a/ several times, making certain it sounds natural and speechlike without inadvertent tongue recruitment and with forward resonance. Sing an /a/ with the cork between the molars on any vocal exercise or current repertoire. Alternate placing the cork on the left or right side molars for symmetry.

Wine Cork

The wine cork is a useful kinesthetic singing tool in the voice studio. Placing a cork between the teeth to disengage jaw tension might seem counterintuitive, but the anecdotal feedback is unequivocally positive. Biologically, the jaw elevator muscles are much stronger than the jaw depressor muscles. This is good news for chewing but not so good for singing. Singing with a wine cork has the following purposes:

- Brings awareness to the antagonism of opposing jaw muscles and of the interconnections between the jaw and tongue muscles that require independent mobility
- Discourages negative antagonism between the opposing jaw muscles while training a neutral, open mouth position
- Serves as a tool to eliminate a component of unwanted jaw engagement and movement
- Encourages a release of unwanted tongue tension that may exist because of the interconnecting structures of the jaw and tongue
- Allows singers to experience a sense of release in the articulators, which leads to efficient voicing
- Facilitates the sensation of forward resonance if unwanted jaw tension is inhibiting an optimal vocal tract shape

Masseter Muscle Release

Purpose 6–4

As previously discussed, the masseter muscle plays a major role in chewing. For those who grind their teeth, the muscle gets extra exercise, which is not necessarily a good thing for a muscle that needs to release unwanted tension when the jaw remains open while singing. Placing the thumbs on the area of the masseter and gently massaging encourages release and discourages the activation of this muscle (Exercise 6–4).

A   **B**

Figure 6–4. Image of singer demonstrating "Masseter Muscle Release" either standing with thumbs placed on the masseter muscle (**A**) or leaning on a piano with the thumbs placed on the masseter muscle (**B**). Be certain the neck remains in a neutral alignment while leaning on the piano.

Exercise 6–4

Locate the top of the masseter muscle by placing each thumb on the underside of the cheekbone notch. Clench until a slight bulge outward reveals the activation of the muscle (Figure 6–4). Massage the masseter by either constant pressure or small kneading circles. Determine a comfortable level of pressure while opening the jaw to about two-fingers width. If additional release is needed, place the elbows on a hard surface (such as a piano) with the thumbs still on the masseter and lean into the thumbs and elbows. If the masseter muscle is tender, adjust the pressure so that it is neither uncomfortable nor inhibits jaw opening. Make certain that the neck remains in good alignment and the chin is not protruding forward. Use the thumbs to gently place pressure on the masseter. Sing vocal exercises or repertoire of your choice.

Tongue Stretches

Tongue Out Stretch

Purpose 6–5 to 6–8

Tongue tension is a universal challenge at some point during a singer's training. Tongue muscles are responsible for extending, elevating, retracting, depressing, and curling actions. They are a very strong group of muscles vital for chewing and swallowing food as well as for speech. The tongue, via the hyoid bone, is connected to the larynx and therefore has profound vocal function implications. Excessive tension in the tongue can impact the vertical position of the larynx (depression or elevation) and therefore vocal function, including resonance strategies. Due to the biological interconnections of the tongue, it is important to condition flexibility, mobility, and independence for efficient singing (Exercises 6–5 to 6–8). Engaging the tongue in stretches prior to singing is an important part of a singer's daily practice regime.

Figure 6–5. Singer demonstrating "Tongue Out Stretch."

 Exercise 6–5

Gently stick the tongue out and direct it downward toward the floor (Figure 6–5). Stretch the tongue as if slowly rolling it off a mounted water hose reel that is oriented from the root of the tongue. Hold this stretch for 8 to 10 s and then release. Repeat the process several times.

Tongue Curl Stretch

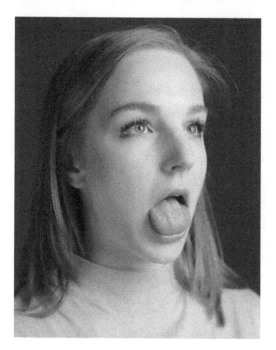

Figure 6–6. Image of singer demonstrating "Tongue Curl Stretch."

 Exercise 6–6

Place the tongue below the inside of the bottom teeth and gently roll the middle of the tongue forward (Figure 6–6). Hold the stretch 8 s to 10 s and then release. Repeat the stretch several times.

Underside of Tongue Stretch

Figure 6–7. Image of singer demonstrating "Underside of Tongue Stretch."

 Exercise 6–7

Anchor the tip of the tongue against the inside of the front teeth. Gently stretch the underside of the tongue forward (Figure 6–7). Hold the stretch for 8 to 10 s and then release. Repeat the stretch several times.

Circular Tongue Stretch

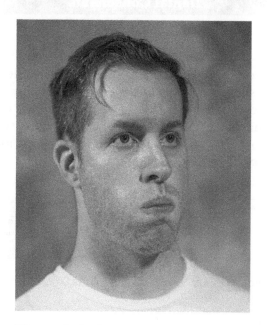

Figure 6–8. Image of a singer demonstrating "Circular Tongue Stretch."

Exercise 6–8

Move the tongue in a 360° circular motion slowly around the outside of the teeth/inside of the lips (Figure 6–8). Begin with a clockwise direction for 10 to 20 repetitions before reversing to a counterclockwise direction. Cue the tongue to release any unwanted tongue root tension during each circular pass. It may fatigue quickly at first and require building to a higher number of circular rotations. It may be useful to massage under the chin while performing this stretch.

Tongue: Voiced Exercises

Dental Consonants

Purpose 6–9

Exercise 6–9 conditions articulatory movement while voicing. The exercise is designed to train independent mobility between the interconnected structures of the jaw and tongue while voicing dental consonants /l/, /d/, /n/, and /t/. This increases awareness of compensatory tongue engagement and develops independence within a variety of tongue movements.

Figure 6–9. Notation for "Dental Consonants."

Exercise 6–9

Using dental consonants /l/, /d/, /n/, and /t/, <u>speak</u> /la-la-la-la-la/, /da-da-da-da-da/, /na-na-na-na-na/, and /ta-ta-ta-ta-ta/. The jaw should be open and released with careful awareness to independent tongue movement. The jaw should remain stationary but not rigid, and the tongue should be liquid and not tense. Sometimes it is necessary to place a hand on the jaw and gently hold it while coordinating the independent movement of the tongue. Sing a five-note scalar pattern using each syllable (Figure 6–9). In a comfortable, low range (C3 males and C4 females), practice the exercise with the syllable of choice. Ascend by half-steps and repeat the exercise to a comfortable high range before descending to the starting pitch. Repeat the exercise using a different syllable or alternate the four dental consonants in one scalar pattern. The tempo is as needed.

Palatal Consonants

Purpose 6–10

The following exercise refers to /k/, /g/, and /j/ as palatal consonants, recognizing that they have more specific names in phonetics.
For this exercise, each consonant is formed by an arched gesture
with the middle of the tongue moving toward the roof of the mouth
and no jaw engagement. This habituates necessary independent
mobility between the tongue and jaw for singing.

Figure 6–10. Notation for "Palatal Consonants."

Exercise 6–10

Using consonants /j/ (pronounced "y" like "yes") /g/, and /k/, speak
the syllables /ja-ja-ja/, /ga-ga- ga/, and /ka-ka-ka/. The tongue will
be liquid while making the gesture toward the roof of the mouth;
the position is slightly more forward than the soft palate. The jaw
should remain stationary but not rigid. Sometimes it is necessary to
gently place a hand on the jaw while coordinating the independent
movement of the tongue. Choose the syllable /ja/, /ga/, or /ka/ and
sing Figure 6–10. Begin in a low range (C3 males and C4 females).
Ascend by half-steps, repeating the exercise to a comfortable high
range. Advance to an arpeggio as shown. Sing a section of current repertoire and replace each word with /ja/. The tongue need
only be in the correct location for this articulatory gesture, but not
tensed or braced. The tempo is as needed.

Developing Jaw and Tongue Independence

Purpose 6–11

As previously discussed, the tongue and jaw interconnections contribute to the swallowing reflex. Exercise 6–11 encourages the antithesis of that tandem action. The vocal task requires the tip of the tongue to remain stationary while simultaneously moving the jaw in a chewing fashion. This disengages potential tandem movement between the two articulators that might impede on a functional singing technique.

Slowly move the jaw while performing this exercise

/n/ _____   /n/ _____

Figure 6–11. Notation for "Developing Jaw and Tongue Independence."

Exercise 6–11

Place the tip of the tongue behind the front teeth and form a dental /n/. The tongue remains liquid, not rigid. Sing /n/ on either melodic pattern shown in Figure 6–11 while slowly moving the jaw in an exaggerated chewing gesture with lips closed. Ascend by half-steps and repeat the exercise. Remain in a comfortable range. When the jaw and tongue have achieved a sense of independence, advance to an octave scale or an arpeggio.

Voiced Raspberry and Tongue Trills

Purpose 6–12

Voiced raspberries and tongue trills are favorite exercises for releasing tongue recruitment (Exercise 6–12). The oscillation of the tongue and necessary coordinated breath management to achieve this task can aid in the habilitation of disengaging unwanted tension. The benefits of raspberries and tongue trills are also discussed in the SOVT section of Chapter 4, the phonation chapter.

Figure 6–12. Notation for "Voiced Raspberry and Tongue Trills."

 Exercise 6–12

Perform either a voiced raspberry (tongue between the lips) or tongue trill as shown in Figure 6–12. The exercise is shown with an arpeggio, but a pitch glide or other scalar pattern may be substituted. Raspberries and tongue trills are very useful during repertoire to ascertain unwanted tongue tension. Perform a section of current repertoire on a raspberry or tongue trill and then repeat the section the words. The voice should sound freer and the singer should report a different kinesthetic sense of articulatory engagement, or lack thereof.

Base of Tongue Disengagement

Purpose 6–13

The thumb can be used to provide a great deal of feedback as to whether the tongue is inadvertently engaged while singing (Exercise 6–13). It is necessary to map the tongue to be in the correct position to form the vowels and consonants but without unwanted recruitment. Often, this exercise reveals unnecessary base of tongue engagement. Using the thumb to massage under the chin while voicing provides a new kinesthetic awareness should the base of the tongue be recruiting or inadvertently depressing while singing.

Figure 6–13. Image of singer demonstrating "Base of Tongue Disengagement."

Exercise 6–13

Before voicing is added to this exercise (Figure 6–13) there is an important four-step process: (1) place the thumb under the middle of the chin and gently massage the base of the tongue; (2) open and close the jaw noticing if the base of the tongue becomes rigid or hard—if so, repeat this step several times, while massaging the area, until the jaw opens and the area under the thumb remains pliable and soft; (3) speak an /a/ and an /i/ several times, making certain the base of the tongue remains soft; (4) chant speech glide (yawn sigh) a high to low pitch on both the /a/ and /i/. The /i/ vowel may take remapping. The tongue must be arched but liquid for the /i/ vowel, and the area under the chin should not be rigid nor should the base of tongue push back against the thumb. Repeat several times. Although some muscle contraction will be felt, it must always be pliable. Once those four steps are mastered, sing a five-note descending scale on an /i/ vowel in the middle range (G5 females and G4 males) while massaging under the chin. Once this is habituated, advance to other scalar patterns.

Candy on the Tongue

Purpose 6–14

The candy exercise brings awareness to tongue activity in order to help singers explore a more released tongue position while singing (Exercise 6–14). The candy provides sensory feedback about unnecessary tongue engagement (see the text box "Candy on the Tongue" below). Although there has never been an issue with aspirating the candy, the author would be remiss not to provide a warning to be careful while using candy as a kinesthetic singing tool.

Figure 6–14. Image of a singer demonstrating "Candy on the Tongue."

Exercise 6–14

Place a small candy on the center of tongue (Figure 6–14). Speak /a/ to assess any tongue recruitment. The vowel should sound natural with a forward, resonant speaking voice. With the candy on the tongue, sing /a/ on an ascending/descending five-note or octave scale. This exercise may be taken to a comfortable upper tessitura. The candy should remain on the center of the tongue. It should not roll around excessively or fall out of the mouth. The candy is also excellent to use while singing repertoire on an /a/ before layering the words back into the process.

Candy on the Tongue

Juilliard Emeritus Ellen Faull used Go Lightly sugar-free butterscotch candy for this exercise. For many reasons, this particular candy remains the author's chosen brand and flavor. Singing while the candy is placed on the center of the tongue has the following purposes:

- Promotes sensory awareness of tongue movement
- Alleviates unnecessary tongue depression, retraction, or elevation
- Encourages a neutral /a/ tongue position
- Helps to stabilize a neutral laryngeal position due to the interconnections between the tongue and its insertion into the larynx at the hyoid bone
- Brings awareness to the relationship between the soft palate and the tongue
- Reminds singers not to depress the tongue while exploring the optimal vocal tract shape, especially for lofted resonance

---

Gauze on the Tongue

Purpose 6–15

Using gauze to hold the tongue facilitates awareness of potential retraction during inhalation and/or singing (Exercise 6–15). Singers must learn to shape the vocal tract for the desired resonance strategy without unnecessary tongue engagement. In particular, classical singers may have a tendency to depress or retract their tongue in an effort to achieve an inverted-megaphone shape (convergent resonator). The gauze material provides an easy way to gently hold the tongue while exploring tongue engagement (see the text box "Gauze on the Tongue" below).

Figure 6–15. Image of a singer demonstrating "Gauze on the Tongue."

 Exercise 6–15

Wrap the gauze around the tip of the tongue, placing the thumb underneath and the pointer finger on top (Figure 6–15). Do not hold the tongue in an outward position beyond the bottom lip. Begin by speaking /a/ several times and bring awareness to any tongue retraction both during inhalation and voicing. Do not sing until release is felt during speaking. The /a/ should sound natural with forward resonance. Yawn-sigh an /a/ glide starting on a pitch around C5 females and C4 males. Repeat a few times, beginning slightly higher with each starting pitch. Notice if the tongue retracts during inhalation or vocal onset and repeat until a release is felt.

Advance to singing vocal exercises or current repertoire on /a/ while holding the tongue with the gauze.

Gauze on the Tongue

The gauze material provides an easy way to gently hold the tongue while singing. This brings kinesthetic awareness of tongue activity to facilitate a positive change in vocal production. Using gauze to hold the tongue while singing has the following purposes:

- Identifies tongue retraction on inhalation
- Identifies tongue retraction during vocal onsets
- Identifies tongue retraction when ascending into the upper range
- Discourages a tongue divot, which unnaturally darkens the tone
- Allows singers to explore the desired vocal tract shape for optimal resonance strategy without unnecessary tongue engagement

---

Ode to Barbara Doscher

Purpose 6–16

The intent of this exercise is not a beautiful tone but, rather, singing with an extremely relaxed jaw, tongue, cheeks, and lips. The cheeks should be encouraged to puff out while producing /pl/ (Exercise 6–16). This exercise is found on a YouTube video posted by John Nix of Barbara Doscher teaching a pedagogy course (https://www.youtube.com/watch?v=K6WeEEilzVc&t=3s).

Puffy cheeks on the /pla/

/pla/　/pla/　/pla/　/pla/　/pla/　/pla/　/pla/　/pla/　/pla/

Figure 6–16. Notation for "Ode to Barbara Doscher."

Exercise 6–16

Sing the syllable /pla/ on a five-note ascending/descending scale (Figure 6–16). Allow the cheeks to puff out during the /pl/ sound. Encourage the tongue, jaw, cheeks, and lips to feel extremely loose. Sing a few scales in comfortable middle range.

Dental/Palatal Consonant Combinations

Purpose 6–17

The tongue must be flexible in order to move in a variety of directions for articulation. Exercise 6–17 uses combinations of dental and palatal consonants in one vocal task to habituate tongue mobility. The tongue needs to be in the correct location for clarity in diction and to form the consonants but should remain liquid in doing so. These exercises encourage movement in the tip, dorsum, and root of the tongue. The jaw may move freely in these exercises, but it should not be excessive. When the tongue is flexible and mobile, vocal function improves.

Figure 6–17. Notation for "Dental/Palatal Consonant Combinations."

Exercise 6–17

Sing a five-note scalar ascending/descending pattern using a combination of dental and palatal consonants as shown in Figure 6–17. Remain in a comfortable midrange until the tongue is acclimated to the patterns. Option 1: The syllables /dɪ-ga/ require quick alternating succession of movement between dental /d/ and palatal /g/ consonants. Option 2: The syllables /gle/-/gla/ use a quick palatal/ dental consonant gesture /gl/ on a single pitch. There are numerous combinations of dental consonants (/l/, /d/, /n/, and /t/) and palatal consonants (/y/, /g/, and /k/) to choose from, depending on the singer's individual needs. Advance to using a combination of sounds on a variety of melodic patterns. The tempo is as needed.

Soft Palate Stretches

Isolating the Soft Palate Activation

Purpose 6–18 A–C

The three stretches in Exercise 6–18 A–C actively engage the muscles of the soft palate. The soft palate is considered the top of the vocal tract and its position contributes significantly to a singer's resonance strategy and quality of sound. By intentionally exploring the range of motion of the soft palate, singers become more familiar with its movement. If a singer is hypernasal, these exercises are crucial.

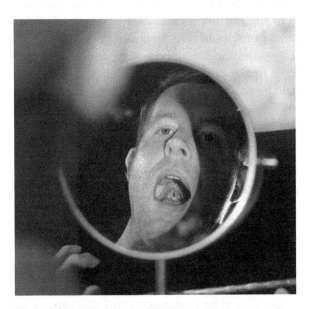

Figure 6–18. Image of singer demonstrating "Isolating the Soft Palate Activation."

Exercise 6–18 A–C

a. Begin by identifying the range of the soft palate motion. Speak the word "hit" and hold the /t/; do not let the tongue release the air. As the tongue is held in place, notice the pressure in the soft palate as the air pushes against its closed position. To experience the opposite sensation, simulate snoring. The soft palate relaxes and flaps about for this activity.

b. The movement of the soft palate is important during blowing and sucking activities. Use a small straw and sip air through it to feel the soft palate activate. Practice this activity when drinking a thick milkshake or smoothie. Place the straw in water (or a thick liquid) and blow to further explore soft palate activation.

c. A mirror is another useful tool (see Figure 6–21 later in this chapter). Begin by fogging up the mirror, blowing on it with an open mouth. This action elevates the soft palate. Next, use a mirror to look inside the mouth and locate the uvula (the thing that dangles down from the back of the roof of the mouth); inhale and encourage the soft palate/uvula area to raise. Be mindful to practice raising the soft palate upon inhalation but not allowing the tongue to depress. Condition your kinesthetic awareness to disengage those two activities, as this separation of movement is necessary for singing.

Soft Palate: Voiced Exercises

Soft Palate Exploration with Voicing

Purpose 6–19

By exploring a myriad of soft palate movements, singers learn to kinesthetically map the sensation of various levels of elevation (Exercise 6–19). This is essential for understanding different sound aesthetics and is critical when hypernasality is present. It is also important that singers map the soft palate movement without tongue depression. For classical singers, the tongue frequently divots in an effort to make perceived "space" in the oral cavity, and those two gestures become inadvertently linked. The soft palate has a natural range of motion for various biological and speaking activities. The voiced exercises should have an aesthetic target. For most repertoires, a CCM singer will have less kinesthetic awareness of soft palate elevation than a classical singer.

/ha/   /ha/   /ha/   /ha/   /ha/   /ha/   /ha/   /ha/

Figure 6–19. Notation for "Soft Palate Exploration with Voicing."

Exercise 6–19

Speak /ha/ with varying degrees of soft palate elevation to explore the range of motion and the aesthetic outcome (Figure 6–19). Repeat several times, noticing the different qualities of sound achieved with the different soft palate positions. Use the /h/ as if fogging up a mirror, then lighten the aspiration to a silent /h/ to promote a balanced onset. Sing four repeated notes in a comfortable range using the same approach. Be mindful of what the tongue is doing throughout this exercise. When exploring a more elevated soft palate, the tongue should not depress or divot.

Using Nasality to Explore the Contrast of Soft Palate Elevation

Purpose 6–20

The nasal /ŋ/ (si**ng**) requires a lowered soft palate and reinforces a sensation of forward resonance in the mouth and nasal cavities. When moving from a nasal consonant (lowered soft palate) to an /a/ (raised soft palate) the contrast between these two sound qualities helps coordinate the correct engagement (Exercise 6–20). The /ŋ/ has the added benefit of facilitating forward resonant sensations.

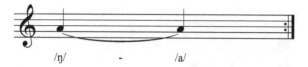

Figure 6–20. Notation for "Using Nasality to Explore the Contrast of Soft Palate Elevation."

Exercise 6–20

Practice saying the word "sing." Map the tongue position of the /ŋ/ so that the middle of the tongue is arched toward the roof of the mouth but is not tensed (see the text box "Mapping the /ŋ/" in Chapter 7, the resonance chapter). Notice the forward resonant sensations on the /ŋ/. Sing /ŋ/-/a/ sustaining a single pitch. Explore a variety of sounds on the /a/ vowel as you vary the elevation of the soft palate (Figure 6–20). This will contribute to changing the aesthetic outcome on a continuum from lofted to brassy resonance. Continue alternating the /ŋ/-/a/ combination staying in a moderate range.

Thumb in Mouth Against the Soft Palate

Purpose 6–21

The thumb can be used to explore movement of the soft palate when inserted toward the back of the roof of the mouth (Exercise 6–21). This proprioceptive awareness can be a powerful experience as singers isolate the intricacies of soft palate elevation and its impact on voice production. This exercise will be most beneficial for a classical aesthetic or a singer with stridency or hypernasality in their tone.

Figure 6–21. Image of singer demonstrating "Thumb in Mouth Against the Soft Palate."

Exercise 6–21

Be certain the singer's hands are sanitized before proceeding. Place the thumb in the mouth and slowly glide it back until arriving at the front of the soft palate where the roof of the mouth begins to become soft (Figure 6–21). Singers with a strong gag reflex may have a problem with this exercise, in which case, they can keep their thumb farther forward and potentially still find kinesthetic benefit. Sing any vocal exercise or current repertoire with the thumb in this position to explore the movement of the soft palate and its impact of the quality of sound.

Summary

The articulatory system is a fascinating contributor to singing. The structures of articulation form a complex and interactive system that have a profound impact on vocal function. Because of the numerous interconnections, it is important to condition as much independence as possible within the system to encourage vocal efficiency.

Reference

McCoy, S. (2012). *Your voice: An inside view* (2nd ed). Delaware, OH: Inside View Press.

Selected Resources

Bozeman, K. (2017). *Kinesthetic voice pedagogy: Motivating acoustic efficiency.* Delaware, OH: Inside View Press.

LeBorgne, W. D., & Rosenberg, M. (2014). *The vocal athlete.* San Diego, CA: Plural Publishing.

McKinney, J. (1994). *The diagnosis & correction of vocal faults: A manual for teachers of singing & for choir directors.* Reissued 2005. Long Grove, IL: Waveland Press.

Miller, R. (1987). Taming the terrible triplets of the vocal tract: Tongue/hyoid bone/larynx. *Journal of Singing, 43*(5), 33–37.

Ragan, K., & Kapsner Smith, M. (2019). Vehicular vocalizing to start your day. *Journal of Voice, 76*(2), 161–166.

Sundberg, J. (1987). *The science of the singing voice.* Dekalb, IL: Northern Illinois University Press.

Titze, I. (1994). *Principles of voice production.* Englewood Cliffs, NJ: Prentice Hall.

Chapter 7

A Systematic Approach to Resonance

The sound of the voice depends on the individual shape of the vocal tract and of the vocal folds as well as on the habitual use of a particular speaker's voice organ. Basically, this fact is well known to all of us; educating and training a voice implies changes in the sound of the voice. Such changes would be impossible to achieve if all voice characteristic were innate.

—Johann Sundberg, *The Science of the Singing Voice* (1987), p. 2

Overview of Resonance

The word resonance is generally defined as the enhancement or amplification of sound (specific frequencies) by supplementary vibration (something beyond the original sound source). What is being amplified or enhanced are the harmonic frequencies that are made by an initial sound source, in this case, the vocal folds. When the vocal folds (source) vibrate at a particular frequency, they produce a sound wave. The sound wave travels into a resonating chamber (filter), in this case the vocal tract, where resonances either enhance or dampen aspects of its properties. In terms of singing, these resonances of the vocal tract (radiated as formants) turn the "buzzing" sounds produced by the vocal folds into a beau tiful and intelligible vocal quality. Resonance is what creates the individuality of the human voice.

195

Sound waves are comprised of the longitudinal motion of the air particles. A percentage of the energy travels out of the mouth toward the audience and a percentage returns to the source. As discussed in Chapter 4, the phonation chapter, resonances of the vocal tract impact the vocal folds either by strengthening or disrupting their vibratory pattern as the sound waves return to the source (inertive or compliant reactance). A descriptive image of this process is that of a child on a swing. The pendulum of the swing moves at a particular frequency or rate of vibration. If the person pushing the swing acts too early or too late, it disrupts the timing of the swing's frequency. When the timing is optimal and at the same rate as the natural frequency, it creates more energy. This is equal to the effects of the vocal tract resonances on the voice source. If resonance in singing is produced in an optimal manner, it creates acoustic energy that helps the vocal folds vibrate more efficiently, resulting in less effortful singing.

Singers can manipulate parts of the vocal tract that shape some of the resonators since movable structures are within their control. The vocal tract is generally described as the area between the glottis and the lips and includes the larynx, pharynx, mouth, and nose (Figure 7–1). Since the vocal tract includes articulators, some of which are moveable (e.g., tongue) and others which are passive (e.g., hard palate), the movable articulators have a tremendous impact on the quality of sound due to their ability to shape the resonating tube (vocal tract).

Interactions between the source harmonics and vocal tract resonances result in acoustic transitions that are experienced by the singer. A comprehensive understanding of *acoustic voice pedagogy* explores how and where these interactions occur and the corresponding sensations experienced by a singer. The complexities of these interactions are beyond the scope of this book, but readers are encouraged to review the selected resources at the end of this chapter.

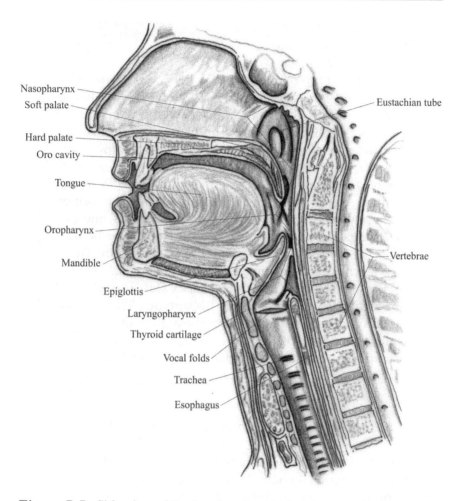

Figure 7–I. Side view of the head and neck showing cavities important to resonance such as the nasopharynx, oropharynx, and laryngopharynx. From *Voice Technique: A Physiologic Approach, Second Edition* (p. 28), by J. E. Bickel, 2017, San Diego, CA: Plural Publishing. Copyright 2018 by Plural Publishing. Used with permission.

Acoustic Voice Pedagogy

Knowledge of the science of singing voice acoustics, perception, and pedagogy can at first seem overwhelming. There are some in the field of voice pedagogy contributing to the accessibility and practical application of this material in the voice studio. Ken Bozeman's books *Practical Vocal Acoustics* and *Kinesthetic Voice Pedagogy* are tremendous resources for enabling voice teachers to more readily understand this complex subject. His seminal work is informed by the physics of vocal acoustics, voice scientists, and earlier voice pedagogues who tackled this subject, as he now distills the information into principles of application. Other voice teachers are gleaning valuable pedagogical applications from studies in psychoacoustics (Ian Howell) and vibrotactile sensation (Chadley Ballantyne). Teachers are encouraged to explore resources through books, articles, seminars, workshops, conferences, and conversations on the important subject of singing voice acoustics.

High-Frequency Spectral Content: Vocal Ring

A resonant voice is often described as one that has achieved a great deal of *vocal ring,* evidenced by the singer's sensation of sympathetic vibrations (mask resonance) in the facial tissue (soft and hard) and the perception of vibrancy of sound to the listener. It is a goal of efficient singing and an indication of effective conversion of aerodynamic energy to acoustic energy (Titze, 2001). *Ring, twang, singer's formant cluster, mask resonance, squillo,* and *brassy* are common terms used to identify vocal ring with significant high frequency harmonic content. The reason that there are so many descriptive words for ring is due to significant timbral differences within genres that, over time, have promoted a variety of labels. In fact, there are distinctive *acoustic* and *physiologic* adjustments responsible for timbral outcomes. In classical singing, squillo, mask resonance, and singer's formant cluster are common terms to describe the presence of ring. Within contemporary commercial music (CCM), the aesthetic of belting often uses descriptors such as twang, bright, or brassy. A good deal of a singer's training is to develop a resonance strategy that enhances specific frequencies to achieve the vibrancy of sound production in the desired aesthetic. This is because a resonant voice indicates a high-intensity sound quality while maintaining low vocal effort that is imperative for vocal health. Ongoing voice research will continue to provide clarity with regard to acoustic and physiological characteristics of the genre-specific ring phenomenon. This will lead to further accuracy of terminology used during voice studio application.

Classical Singer's Lofted Resonance Strategy

The *singer's formant cluster* is associated with vocal ring in Western classical singing technique. Voice scientists have studied acoustic, physiologic, and perceptual parameters responsible for this quality. It is a unique resonance strategy with a harmonic peak created by a clustering of acoustic energy of the third, fourth, and fifth formants at a frequency range of 2500 to 3500 Hz to achieve a ring that gives extra amplification to the voice (Sundberg, 1974). This boost of acoustic energy (resonance) is experienced as dynamic sound waves to the listener and is associated as sympathetic vibrations in the facial tissue, sometimes called the mask or mask resonance.

The singer's formant cluster is achieved with a narrowing of the epilarynx tube (a portion of the cavity of the larynx between the vocal folds and the top of the epiglottis) and a wider pharynx (Estill, Fujimura, Sawada, & Beechler-Obert, 1996) (Figure 7–11). The narrowing of the small resonating tube (epilarynx) within the larger vocal tract tube (pharynx) essentially becomes a resonator within a resonator that boosts the harmonics in the singer's formant. To achieve this resonance strategy, the exit of the smaller tube must be less than one-sixth the size of the surrounding vocal tract (Sundberg, 1974). Along with other factors (e.g., vocal fold configuration, vocal tract shape, vertical laryngeal position), the narrowing of the epilarynx and wider pharynx achieves a rich and robust sound that maintains the perception of a ringing quality. This vocal production is associated with operatic singing.

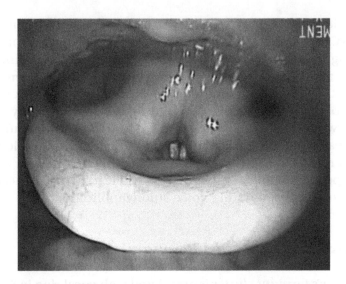

Figure 7–II. Endoscopic view of the larynx and surrounding structures, including the epiglottis. The image shows a narrow epilarynx tube as seen in the production of the singer's formant cluster. Shared with the permission of Kerrie Obert and Karen Perta.

CCM Singer's Brassy Resonance Strategy

On the other end of the continuum is a brassy resonance strategy. The term twang is common nomenclature used to describe a brassy quality associated with ring and found within the broad spectrum CCM, including musical theatre, pop, rock, and country. A discussion of terminology with regard to twang can be confusing because it identifies two very different vocal productions: *nasal twang* and *oral twang*. A primary physiologic difference between nasal and oral twang is the degree to which the soft palate (velum) is lowered or raised. Since both nasal and oral twang encourage a brassy, resonant sensation, it is possible to confuse actual nasal resonance achieved with a lowered soft palate (nasal twang) with the resonance achieved with a raised soft palate (oral twang) (Yanagisawa, Estill, Kmucha, & Leder, 1989). For nasal twang, acoustic energy is propagated through the nasal cavity and creates, in varying degrees, a perceptual nasal or "honky" quality. Nasal twang is often associated with country music and some character voices. In this book, twang refers to oral twang with minimal or no nasalized sound, rather a bright, brassy, ringy quality often associated with a belt aesthetic.

Early studies indicate that the brighter sound production of twang was the result of a narrowing of a nonspecific region of the pharynx, with most studies pointing to the epilarynx. It is stated that twang is a quality produced by a narrow pharynx and a narrow epilarynx tube, which raises the first formant (resonance of the vocal tract) and brightens the vowel (Sundberg & Thalén, 2010; Titze, & Verdolini Abbott, 2012, p. 288) (Figure 7–III). Kerrie Obert provided specificity to the ongoing research by noting a pharyngeal wall narrowing (supralaryngeal area) at the level of the middle constrictor as being the primary contributor to shaping the pharynx and creating the sound identified as twang. Her extensive research on this topic was presented at the Estill World Voice Symposium in Quebec, Canada, in the summer of 2017 with copresenter Karen Perta and is currently in press.

Following Obert's research, Chadley Ballantyne suggested an acoustic theory during a NATS Chat (Obert & Ballantyne, 2019) that will be presented in a forthcoming paper. Ballantyne states:

> Twang is acoustic energy above 5000 Hz (Titze, 2001). Pharyngeal narrowing creates twang. When the pyriform sinuses are exposed in a released pharynx, they act as anti-resonances and attenuate acoustic energy above 4000 Hz or 5 kHz (Dang & Honda, 1997). This attenuation, or dip, is the pyriform sinus notch (Ternström, 2008). When the pharyngeal walls constrict or narrow, they cover the pyriform sinuses (Figure 7–IV). When pharyngeal narrowing covers the pyriform sinuses, the pyriform sinus notch goes away, and we have acoustic energy above 5000 Hz in the radiated spectrum. When singers use twang, they are amplifying high harmonics well above the fundamental frequency in the complex soundwave. (C. Ballantyne, personal communication, August 24, 2019)

This is different from vocal ring, identified as the singer's formant cluster at the 2500 to 3500 Hz range. In other words, the aesthetic of vocal ring often described as twang is neither the same physiologic production nor acoustic outcome as the vocal ring recognized in Western classical singing. Regardless of the labels chosen by voice teachers to identify vocal ring within specific genres, this is an important distinction.

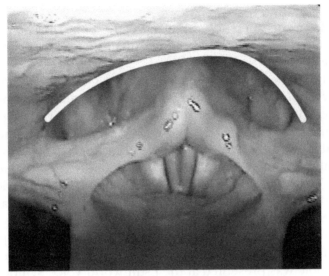

A

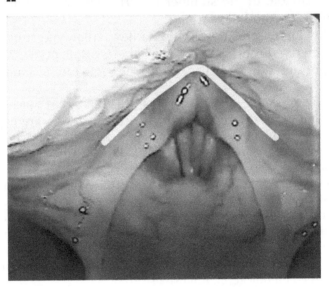

B

Figure 7–III. Endoscopic view of the larynx and the surrounding structures. The images show a wider pharyngeal wall (*white line*) with the open pyriform sinus (**A**) and the narrower pharyngeal wall (**B**) as observed during a belt (*twang*) aesthetic. Shared with the permission of Kerrie Obert and Karen Perta.

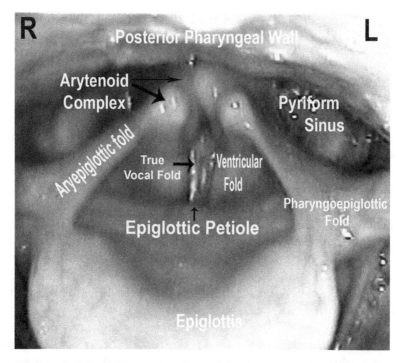

Figure 7–IV. Endoscopic view of the larynx and surrounding structures (including pyriform sinus) as observed from above the closed vocal folds. Adapted from *Clinical Voice Pathology: Theory and Management* (6th ed., p. 18), by J. C. Stemple, N. Roy, and B. K. Klaben, 2020, San Diego, CA: Plural Publishing. Copyright 2020 by Plural Publishing. Used with permission.

Using twang as part of training the high-intensity vocal production of a belt aesthetic has important vocal health implications. Research has revealed that formant differences (resonances) are more important than source differences (greater closed quotient) for the perception of twang (Sundberg & Thalèn, 2010). Training singers to skillfully achieve twang increases efficient singing that is powerful, while decreasing vocal effort (Guzman et al., 2015; Titze, 2008). This is important since singers want to use optimal resonance strategies to achieve a longer closed phase with less vocal fold compression for high-intensity singing. Using the resonance strategy required of oral twang to inform the belt aesthetic may afford CCM singers the ability to perform several shows a week without vocal health concerns that arise from sustaining this high-intensity vocal production.

Western Classical Versus CCM

Regardless of labels, developing vocal resonance is a desired outcome, since the goal of high-intensity singing, such as opera or belting, is to achieve high vocal efficiency with low vocal effort. As discussed in Chapter 5, the registration chapter, adjustments are made to the vibrational mode of the vocal folds on a continuum from chest voice (high closed quotient, increased vertical phase difference, and high amplitude of vibration) to head voice (high open quotient, reduced vertical phase difference, and low amplitude of vibration). This chapter focuses on acoustics while acknowledging that there is a broad continuum of vocal qualities between the extremes of lofted and brassy resonance.

A lofted resonance strategy for classical singing is produced by a lengthened vocal tract, convergent resonator (inverted-megaphone), wider pharyngeal space, and neutral-low laryngeal position; the fundamental frequency and/or the singer's formant cluster carries the acoustic energy. A brassy resonance strategy for the belt aesthetic is achieved by a shortened vocal tract, divergent resonator (megaphone), narrower pharynx, and neutral-high laryngeal position; the energy above the fundamental frequency dominates the sound spectrum. The slide rule analogy discussed in Chapter 5, the registration chapter (see Figure 5–III), is useful in visualizing the potential for a variety of aesthetic possibilities. While all of these parameters impact the outcome of the quality of sound, a singer's kinesthetic sense of resonance, vocal ring, becomes the great unifier.

Teacher Takeaways

Broadly speaking, the term resonance can mean many things. In terms of voice, it has a perceptual meaning. It also has a meaning in physics, referring to a reinforcement of vibration or, more specifically, sound through the reflection of waves (recall vocal tract inertance). Two broad voice teacher takeaways at the core of this information are that harmonic frequencies produced by the vocal folds travel through the vocal tract and (1) impact the output of the quality of sound (source-filter model) and (2) return to the source of the sound (vocal folds) to influence the vibratory pattern in either a positive or negative manner (inertive or compliant reactance). Singers often experience inertance as sympathetic vibrations in the facial tissue, sometimes called the *mask* or *mask resonance*. Attention to these sensations can be enormously helpful at guiding singers toward a secure vocal production. It is, however, important to note that "the vibrations in and of themselves are not the resonance; they are a byproduct of an *interaction resonance* between the source and the vocal tract" (Titze & Verdolini Abbott, 2012, p. 288).

As discussed in the articulation chapter, singers can manipulate parts of the vocal tract that shape some of the resonators since movable structures are within their control. They include the tongue, lips, jaw, palate, pharynx, and larynx. These structures shape resonances and contribute to the desired sound quality. With regard to the application of these principles, understanding the interconnections between the articulators, which contribute to resonance, is paramount to voice teaching because they profoundly impact both a functional singing technique and contribute to achieving the desired aesthetic.

Sensory feedback is essential to the process of resonance explorations. Singers produce both *forced resonance* and *free resonance*. There are physical sensations created by forced resonance; however, they are quickly dampened by body tissue. McCoy calls these a singer's private resonance because they are experienced differently by the individual and therefore may be less reliable in teaching (McCoy, 2012, p. 26). Free resonance requires the hollow spaces in the vocal tract and is what the audience hears. Free resonance is what voice teachers spend time collaboratively developing with their students. The challenge is that singers must contend with at least two sources of feedback systems: external auditory feedback (perception of the acoustics of the room) and internal feedback (the bodies' sensory system) (Helding, 2017). The listener's ears (audience or teacher) are also significantly impacted by the acoustics of the room and equally so by the expertise of the listener. This creates a unique dance between the student and teacher to ascertain, through many perceptual qualities, how to guide efficient and artistic singing.

Application of Resonance

The following exercises are intended to guide singers toward the kinesthetic exploration of resonance. Using these exercises as a roadmap, voice teachers will guide the singer toward the desired aesthetic, making any necessary alterations to resonance strategy along the way. It is important that singers are cognizant of the prephonatory intention, which simply means imagining the sound before it is produced. This can be thought of as the simple cue "shape before you phonate." Singing begins in the mind of the singer; this mental and resultant physical preparation is essential to a successful outcome.

When exploring resonance, there is a conventional approach to using nasalized phonemes such as /m/, /n/, and /ŋ/ to kinesthetically guide singers. These sounds tend to encourage sympathetic vibrations experienced in the facial tissue. Nasalized sounds, although performed with a lowered soft palate, can encourage important sensory feedback due to the perception of forward resonant sensations experienced by the singer. Designing exercises using /m/, /n/, and /ŋ/ preceding a vowel is frequently successful in voice training and an ideal place to begin. Exercises in this chapter to facilitate forward resonance not patterned after nasalized sounds are influenced by Arthur Lessac's Y-buzz and Chadley Ballantyne's retroflex /ɻ/. This chapter introduces one kinesthetic singing tool: a chopstick.

The author recognizes that there is gender diversity. Therefore, when exercises are referenced as being suitable for the male or female voice, nonbinary and/or transitioning singers may refer to whichever exercise or pitch range is most suitable for their vocal development. Vocal exercises must always be altered for the individual needs of the singer.

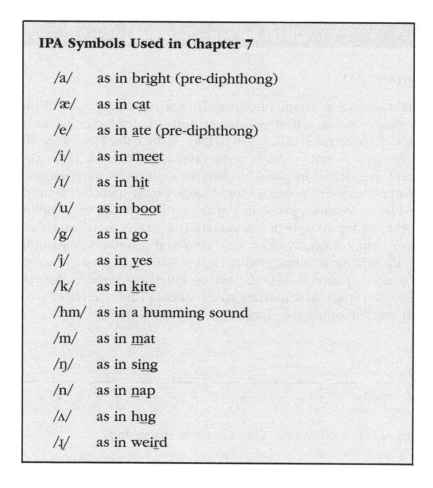

IPA Symbols Used in Chapter 7

/a/   as in br<u>i</u>ght (pre-diphthong)

/æ/   as in c<u>a</u>t

/e/   as in <u>a</u>te (pre-diphthong)

/i/   as in m<u>ee</u>t

/ɪ/   as in h<u>i</u>t

/u/   as in b<u>oo</u>t

/g/   as in <u>g</u>o

/j/   as in <u>y</u>es

/k/   as in <u>k</u>ite

/hm/   as in a humming sound

/m/   as in <u>m</u>at

/ŋ/   as in si<u>ng</u>

/n/   as in <u>n</u>ap

/ʌ/   as in h<u>u</u>g

/ɻ/   as in wei<u>r</u>d

Figure 7–V. Image of a keyboard with pitch notation.

Chant Speech—Humming

Purpose 7–1

Chant speech is frequently used by voice therapists to facilitate forward resonance, flow phonation, and reduced laryngeal tension. It has demonstrated efficacy in helping reduce the phonatory effort that results in symptoms of voice fatigue (McCabe & Titze, 2002). Chant speech was inspired by chanting-style music and therefore is a natural segue to exercises for singers. Chant speech is character-ized by a rhythmic, prosodic pattern and a reciting of syllables or words in a legato style of monopitch. The goal of this exercise is the kinesthetic continuity of forward *and* oral resonance, encouraged by alternating humming with each vowel to facilitate consistent vibrations (Exercise 7–1). Increased lofted resonance, created by more oral space, is important to the intent of this exercise (see the text box "Mapping the /hm/" later in this chapter").

Figure 7–1. Notation for "Chant Speech—Humming."

Exercise 7–1

The symbol /hm/ is used by this author to imply a humming sound, with more oral space and oral resonance than is produced on /m/. To produce /hm/ the intraoral space is to be mapped as if shaped for an /a/ with the lips lightly closed for the /m/ around the openness of the vowel. The /h/ is silent but is used to encour-age airflow. Chant speech the pattern notated in Figure 7–1 to explore forward and oral resonant sensations. Linger on the /hm/ so that it is given *equal* time to that of each vowel. Repeat several times until resonance is experienced as one continuous sound produced throughout the chant exercise. Once the chant speech is established, sing the same pattern on a single pitch in a comfort-able low range as notated in the second part of Figure 7–1. There should be a great deal of consistent, sympathetic vibratory sensations experienced throughout this exercise. Ascend by half-steps and repeat the exercise.

Mapping the /hm/

The author has chosen /hm/ to represent increased oral resonance achieved through a vocal tract shape that is taller (convergent resonator) than might be experienced by /m/ (used in previous exercises). The internal oral cavity shape of /hm/ should be that of a lofted, open, vibrant /a/ with the lips lightly closed around that space. There is to be no tension in the oral cavity (e.g., lips, tongue, cheeks, floor of the mouth) or jaw. Sympathetic vibrations will be experienced as both forward and oral resonance. Make certain the tongue dorsum is not pressing down in an effort to create "tall" space in the vocal tract but is instead floating freely in the mouth. Explore humming throughout the tessitura noticing forward and oral resonant sensations.

Pitch Glides—Humming

Purpose 7–2

The benefits of pitch glides and SOVT exercises were outlined in Chapter 4, the phonation chapter. Exercise 7–2 combines both vocal gestures as well as humming /hm/ (SOVT) and pitch glides to encourage the kinesthetic awareness of forward and oral resonance (see the text box "Mapping the /hm/" above).

Figure 7–2. Notation for "Pitch Glides—Humming."

Exercise 7–2

Begin in a low middle range using /hm/ while slowly pitch gliding an ascending/descending interval of a 3rd, 5th, or an octave (Figure 7–2). As outlined in the previous exercise, the /h/ is silent and the /hm/ symbol indicates oral cavity space through a tall vowel. Allow the voice to naturally transition from chest registration to head registration when necessary. Depending on the desired aesthetic, maintaining a light chest registration for females above the first register transition may be a beneficial use for this exercise, or alternate between chest and head registration. Singers can also explore a variety of vocal tract configurations while humming.

Using /hm/ to Facilitate Resonance

Purpose 7–3

Exercise 7–3 builds on the previous two exercises by adding stepwise intervals to encourage the training of consistence resonance across a variety of vocal patterns. Beyond the benefits already outlined, this exercise brings awareness to excessive jaw movement that might impede a consistent resonance strategy.

Figure 7–3. Notation for "Using /hm/ to Facilitate Resonance."

Exercise 7–3

Sing the pattern shown in Figure 7–3 using the /hm/ previously outlined. It is important to monitor excessive jaw movement; the jaw should not move when the vowel remains the same during the changing pitch of a major third. There are a couple of ways to alter the design of this exercise depending on the needs of the singer: (1) sing a descending 5-3-4-2-3-1-2-7-1 pattern for singers who tend toward too heavy a chest mechanism or (2) alter the starting vowel to /a/ instead of /i/ if an open vowel is more advantageous than a closed vowel at the vocal onset. This exercise is for the middle range and should begin around C4 (females) and C3 (males) and ascend by half-steps to approximately an octave higher.

Mapping the /ŋ/

The velar nasal consonant /ŋ/ (as in the "ng" of si<u>ng</u>) requires specificity in mapping the position of the tongue and jaw for singing. The tongue is arched toward the middle of the roof of the mouth (more fronted) rather than farther back at the soft palate. The tongue makes contact with the roof of the mouth but should be "liquid" with no tension while acquiring this position. The jaw is to hang slightly open in a neutral, free position. Say the word "sing" several times, lingering on the /ŋ/ to explore a kinesthetic sense of the tongue position and the vibrations in the facial tissue.

Ode to Ellen Faull

Purpose 7–4

This exercise was used extensively by Juilliard Emeritus Ellen Faull. It is excellent for coordinating many aspects of articulation and resonance. By alternating nasalized consonants (/ŋ/, /n/, /m/) and vowels (/i/, /a/), singers will experience a continuity in resonance strategy (Exercise 7–4). The nasal consonants promote consistency of forward resonance (see the text box "Mapping the /ŋ/" above).

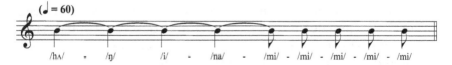

Figure 7–4. Notation for "Ode to Ellen Faull."

Exercise 7–4

Begin with a subtle /h/ (not overly aspirate) followed by a vibrant vowel on /hʌ/ (hung) before closing to /ŋ/ by moving the dorsum of the tongue to an arched position in the middle of the roof of the mouth; continue to the /i/ with very little change in the tongue position; then sing the /n/ with only the tip of the tongue without jaw movement; conclude with /mi/ (Figure 7–4). The kinesthetic sense of forward resonance should continue throughout the progression including the /ŋ/, /n/, and /m/. Give equal time to the vowel and the consonant. This exercise is for the middle range and should begin around B4 (female) and B3 (males) and descend by half-steps until approximately an octave lower. The tongue needs to be in the correct position but should remain "liquid" throughout the exercise.

Alternating /m/ with a Vowel Series

Purpose 7–5

This exercise facilitates resonance in the middle vocal range as a baseline of efficient sound production (Exercise 7–5). It is important to establish resonant sensations in this tessitura previous to singing a higher range. Alternating /m/ with each vowel facilitates consistent resonant sensations.

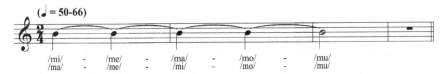

Figure 7–5. Notation for "Alternating /m/ with a Vowel Series."

Exercise 7–5

This exercise is intended for the middle range and should begin around C5 (female) and C4 (males) and descend by half-steps until approximately an octave lower. The series of syllables can be altered from /mi/-/me/-/ma/-/mo/-/mu/ to /ma/-/me/-/mi/-/mo/-/mu/ depending on the individual needs of the singer (Figure 7–5). Use the /m/ to promote resonance in between each vowel. Descend by half-steps to a comfortably low note. Depending on the desired aesthetic, the resonance strategy can be altered through the shape of the vowel: a taller more rounded vowel versus a speechlike vowel.

Bending Forward

Purpose 7–6

When singers find it challenging to access a feeling of forward resonance, leaning forward at the hips so that the body is either parallel to the floor or at a slight angle can facilitate awareness of these sensations (Exercise 7–6). Leaning forward has the added benefit of encouraging abdominal wall release (toward the floor) and expansion of the rib cage upon inhalation for efficient breath management.

/m/ - /u/

A

B

Figure 7–6. A. Notation for "Bending Forward."
B. Image of "Bending Forward" exercise.

Exercise 7–6

Bend at the hips to a 90° angle so the body is parallel to the floor with the arms resting on the piano and the forehead resting on the forearms. This position provides stability to the postural muscles. Make certain the spine stays lengthened and the neck feels comfortably supported. Sing /m/ followed by an /u/ as shown in Figure 7–6. Use the /m/ to promote forward resonance preceding each vowel. Depending on the desired aesthetic, the resonance strategy can be altered through the shape of the vowel: a taller more rounded vowel versus a speechlike vowel. This exercise is for the middle vocal range. The goal is to have a strong kinesthetic sense of sympathetic vibrations in the facial tissue (mask).

Lying Over a Ball

Purpose 7–7

Although the following exercise may seem unusual, it is extremely useful in helping singers experience forward resonance and free vocal production. Lying over a large exercise ball helps to turn off postural muscles that may try to "contribute" to the voice turning over, particularly in the secondo passaggio (Exercise 7–7). For singers finding it challenging to experience forward resonant sensations, this exercise provides significant kinesthetic feedback toward sympathetic vibrations and efficiency in voice production.

A

Figure 7–7. A. Notation for "Lying over a Ball."
continues

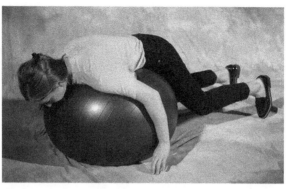

B

Figure 7–7. *continued* **B.** Image of singer "Lying over a Ball." It is imperative that the chin is resting on the ball and that the neck achieves neutral alignment during the exercise. Singers can also choose to roll quite a bit more forward than this picture shows.

Exercise 7–7

Finding the correct position lying across the large exercise ball is crucial to the success of this exercise. Start by kneeling in front of the ball and then gradually lying across it. Once balance is acquired, explore resting the chin on the ball (Figure 7–7B). It is critical that the position of the neck/larynx is neutral once the chin is resting on the ball. From this position, roll the ball forward, allowing the head to be lower than the shoulders at whatever degree is best for the individual. Sing the melodic pattern notated in Figure 7–7A on either a resonant /u/ or "Y-buzz" (see the text box "Y-buzz" later in this chapter). This exercise is for the middle range between F4–F5 (females) and E3–E4 (males).

Chopstick Between the Teeth

Purpose 7–8

Placing a chopstick between the teeth provides a visual tool for imagining sound that is directed over the top of the implement.

This can be useful in facilitating forward resonance. The chopstick also gives tactile feedback for the tongue position. This exercise was used extensively by Ellen Faull, Juilliard emeritus, because it is useful in guiding singers toward the kinesthetic sense of vocal ring.

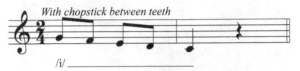

A

B

Figure 7–8. A. Notation for "Chopstick Between the Teeth." **B.** Image of singer demonstrating "Chopstick Between the Teeth."

Exercise 7–8

Gently hold the chopstick between the teeth. Begin by speaking /i/. Make certain the tongue is arched and liquid for the /i/ vowel, but not rigid. The tip of the tongue should remain against the bottom front teeth. Speak /i/ several times until forward resonance is achieved without unwanted tongue tension in the tip or dorsum. Sing the exercise notated in Figure 7–8 with the same forward, resonant sensations. This exercise is not intended for a high tessitura and should remain between C4–F5 (females) and C3–F4 (males), unless the singer is skilled at vowel modification on an /i/ vowel. Ascend by half-steps to a comfortably high note, modifying the /i/ to an /ɪ/ in the upper range, as necessary. While singing through the secondo passaggio, the exercise may require holding the chopstick to allow the jaw more opening.

Resonant Voice Method from Speech Therapy

Resonant voice therapy also known as Lessac-Madsen Resonant Voice Therapy (LMRVT) is a technique widely used in voice clinics to facilitate oral sensations of forward resonance. Speech-language pathologists who specialize in voice have training in implementing this method. Resonant voice exercises decrease vocal fold contact force (adduction) and minimize pressure needed to produce voice. The goal is to feel a "buzzy" sensation in the front of the mouth/face during voicing. This method of voice therapy has undergone thorough research to support its efficacy (Verdolini, 1998, 2000), thus exemplifying the benefits of a multidisciplinary approach to voice teaching. The development of exercises to facilitate efficient voicing for speech and singing can be adapted across disciplines.

Chadley's "Weird" /ɻ/ Exercise

Purpose 7–9

An American retroflex /ɻ/ (as in the word weird) can be used as a sound to guide singers toward the kinesthetic sensations of resonance. Chadley Ballantyne presented a compelling explanation through acoustic demonstration at the Pan-American Vocology Association's (PAVA) Third Annual Symposium in October 2017. He outlined the use of the retroflex /ɻ/ in the book *The Evolving Singing Voice* (Brunssen, 2018) and discussed this concept on the October 2018 *NATS Chat* webinar. In essence, when formants are close together in the spectrum, they boost each other (Sundberg, 1974). This occurs when using the retroflex /ɻ/ (in this case the second and third formants). Exercise 7–9 utilizes the benefits of /ɻ/ prior to an /a/ to guide resonant sensations, resulting in more vocal power and unification. It also encourages tongue flexibility and mobility by establishing sensations of the interactions between articulation, respiration, and resonation.

/wi/ - /ɻ/   /a/

Figure 7–9. Notation for "Chadley's "Weird" /ɻ/ Exercise."

Exercise 7–9

The following exercise is informed and inspired by Chadley Ballantyne's "weird" /ɻ/ exercise. For even greater detail, see Brunssen, 2018, p. 284.

1. Begin by saying words that end with an America /ɻ/ such as far, ear, and bar. Linger on the /ɻ/
2. Begin to sustain a pitch when speaking those words by emphasizing the /ɻ/. Notice the resonant sensations created in this process. It may take time to explore the tongue position to amplify the potentially "buzzy" feeling of the /ɻ/.
3. On a sustained pitch, in a resonant voice, slowly speak the word "weird" /wwwwwiiiiiiiiiiiɻɻɻɻɻɻɻɻ/ (drop the /d/).
4. In a comfortable middle range, sing a sustained pitch on /wi_ɻɻɻɻɻɻ_aaaaaaa/, adding /a/ or /o/ to the pattern.
5. Use the "weird" pattern of lingering on the /ɻ/ to precede an /a/ and continue singing an ascending/descending three-note

or five-note scale (Figure 7–9). Ascend by half-steps through the passaggio. Singers should notice more clarity and vocal ring in the voice.

Y-Buzz

Purpose 7–10

Inspired by Arthur Lessac's Y-buzz, Exercise 7–10 encourages forward resonance by means of a nonnasalized sounds. Lessac felt the conventional approach to voice building through nasal consonants /m/, /n/, and /ŋ/ was not the proper model for optimal voice production (Lessac, 1997, pp. 122–141). Although he does acknowledge that there is nothing wrong with nasal consonants and that they add color and musicality to speech, he believed that patterning voice development after intrinsically nasal sounds could lead to a somewhat strident or unpleasant sound in the speaking voice. The Y-buzz is one of Lessac's many techniques that are used in a holistic, kinesensic approach. The Y-buzz uses a nonnasal model through a sustained "Y" to encourage forward resonant sensations in speech. This exercise is inspired by Lessac and adapted for singers. For classical singers familiar with foreign language diction, the sound is close to a French /y/ (but is more rounded).

Figure 7–10. Notation for "Y-Buzz."

Exercise 7–10

Begin with lips in a /ʃ/ ("sh") as if telling someone to be quiet. Keep the lips in this position and place the tongue in a "y" as if about to say the word "ye." Encourage a lengthened vocal tract (inverted megaphone shape). In this position, chant speech "ye" with slightly rounded lips, being certain that there is no tension in the tongue or lips. Alternate the "y" with /i/ so that both sounds are present in a unique, rounded, resonant vibration. The sound should have a sense of forward resonance without any nasality. Explore the sensations through the front teeth, hard palate, cheekbones, forehead, top of the head, and even the chest cavity. Continue exploring where sympathetic vibrations may be felt by gliding the pitch up and down, staying in the lower third of the speaking range during this phase. Advance the Y-buzz speech glides to singing a five-note ascending/descending scale (Figure 7–10). Next, add an /a/ to the scale following the Y-buzz, maintaining the resonant sensations previously achieved (see Figure 7–10).

Facilitating Brassy Resonance (Twang)

Purpose 7–11 A–C

As outlined earlier in this chapter, oral twang is a term indicating a brassy resonance found in CCM genres. When produced correctly, it facilitates an efficient voice and minimizes potential hyperfunction. There may be slight nasality when first exploring twang, but nasality is not the goal. The goal of twang is a bright, brassy sound, but it is not achieved by making the voice louder; rather, that is the outcome when efficiently produced. The goal of Exercise 7–11 A–C is kinesthetic sensations of twang that are perceived as brassy resonance. It may be useful to incorporate playful, funny sounds when first exploring twang. Common prompts used in the voice studio are "baaaaa"-ing like a sheep, cackling like a witch, "yæ-hæ-hæ," or the childhood taunt "nyæ" used in a melodic tone 5-5-3-6-5-3. (This IPA symbol /æ/ indicates a bright vowel sound found in the word "brat" or "cat.")

Figure 7–11A. Notation for "Facilitating Brassy Resonance (Twang)."

Exercise 7–11 A

After exploring twang through the vocal gestures above, apply the same resonance strategy to singing /njæ/ (sound like "nyae") as shown in Figure 7–11A. It is useful to map the movement of the tongue for the gesture of the "ny." The /n/ is produced with the tip of the tongue gently behind the front teeth; the tongue dorsum then gently rolls to the roof of the mouth to find the gesture of the "y" followed by /æ/. Do not brace or press the tongue in an effort to achieve twang. That has the potential to create unwanted tension or laryngeal elevation. The range will be dependent upon the ability to maintain a chest-dominant registration with brassy resonance.

Figure 7–11B. Notation for "Facilitating Brassy Resonance (Twang)."

Exercise 7–11 B

Sing the word "sing," sustaining the /ŋ/ at the end of the word and perform the pattern in Figure 7–11B. Be certain that the tongue is not braced or unnecessarily tensed while habituating the brassy resonance of twang. There is a great deal of forward resonance experienced in the facial tissue. The /s/ is used to encourage breath energy. The range will be dependent upon the ability to maintain a chest-dominant registration with brassy resonance.

Figure 7–11C. Notation for "Facilitating Brassy Resonance (Twang)."

Exercise 7–11 C

Use /ŋ/ ("ng") as the continuation of twang in between the vowels /i/, /æ/, and /a/ as shown in Figure 7–11C. There is a great deal of forward resonance experienced in both the /ŋ/ and vowels. Be certain that the tongue is not braced or tensed while habituating the brassy resonance of twang. The range will be dependent upon the ability to maintain a chest-dominant registration with brassy resonance throughout the exercise.

Summary

Resonance is the byproduct of a process that uses the buzzing tones made by vocal fold vibrations and changes it into beautiful sound. The individuality of the human voice is created in this transformation. To achieve resonance for the desired aesthetic outcome requires a complex series of events that take time to master. Acquiring optimal resonance is also an indication of efficient singing that has important vocal health implications. Pedagogical knowledge of how harmonics are likely to interact with resonance frequencies (radiated as formants) provides clarity in teaching strategies. Readers are encouraged to explore that knowledge in detail. The ultimate goal is to produce beautiful, artistic sounds that promote expressive singing and engage the listener.

References

Brunssen, K. (2018). *The evolving singing voice: Changes across the lifespan*. San Diego, CA: Plural Publishing.

Dang, J., & Honda, K. (1997). Acoustic characteristics of the piriform fossa in models and humans. *The Journal of the Acoustical Society of America, 101*(1), 456–465.

Estill, J., Fujimura, O., Sawada, M., & Beechler-Obert, K. (1996). Temporal perturbation and voice qualities. In P. J. Davis & N. H. Fletcher (Eds.), *Vocal fold physiology: Controlling complexity and chaos* (pp. 237–252). San Diego, CA: Singular Publishing.

Guzman, M., Lanas, A., Olavarria, C., Azocar, M., Muñoz, D., Madrid, S., . . . Mayerhoff, R. (2015). Laryngoscopic and spectral analysis of laryngeal and pharyngeal configuration in non-classical singing styles. *Journal of Voice, 29*(1), 130.e21–130.e28.

Helding, L. (2017). Cognitive dissonance: Facts versus alternative facts. *Journal of Singing, 74*(1), 89–93.

Lessac, A. (1997). *The use and training of the human voice: A biodynamic approach to vocal life* (3rd ed.). Mountain View, CA: Mayfield Publication.

McCabe, D., & Titze, I. (2002). Chant therapy for treating vocal fatigue among public school teachers: A preliminary study. *American Journal of Speech-Language Pathology, 11*(4), 356–369.

McCoy, S. (2012). *Your voice: An inside view* (2nd ed.). Delaware, OH: Inside View Press.

Obert, K., & Ballantyne, C. (2019). *NATS chat: Getting the twang of it* [Video file]. Retrieved from https://www.youtube.com/watch?v=KHjbqUYrb04&feature=youtube

Sundberg, J. (1974). Articulatory interpretation of the "singing formant." *Journal of American Statistical Association, 55*, 838–844.

Sundberg, J., & Thalén, M. (2010). What is twang? *Journal of Voice, 24*(6), 654–660.

Ternström, S. (2008). Hi-Fi voice: Observations on the distribution of energy in the singing voice spectrum above 5 kHz. *Journal of the Acoustical Society of America, 123*(5), 3171–3176.

Titze, I. R. (2001). Acoustic interpretation of resonant voice. *Journal of Voice, 15*(4), 519–528.

Titze, I., & Verdolini Abbott, K. (2012). *Vocology: The science and practice of voice habilitation.* Salt Lake City, UT: National Center for Voice and Speech.

Verdolini, K. (1998). *Resonant voice therapy.* Iowa City, IA: The National Center for Voice and Speech.

Verdolini, K. (2000). Resonant voice therapy. In J. C. Stemple (Ed.), *Voice therapy: Clinical studies* (2nd ed., pp. 46–62). San Diego, CA: Singular Publishing.

Yanagisawa, E., Estill, J., Kmucha, S. T., & Leder, S. B. (1989). The contribution of aryepiglottic constriction to "ringing" voice quality. *Journal of Voice, 3*(4), 342–350.

Selected Resources

Bozeman, K. (2013). Acoustic passaggio pedagogy for the male voice. *Logopedics Phoniatrics Vocology, 38*(2), 64–69.

Bozeman, K. (2013). *Practical vocal acoustics: Pedagogic applications for teachers and singers.* Hillsdale, NY: Pendragon Press.

Bozeman, K. (2017). *Kinesthetic voice pedagogy: Motivating acoustic efficiency.* Delaware, OH: Inside View Press.

Howell, I. (2016). *Parsing the spectral envelope: Toward a general theory of vocal tone color* (Doctoral dissertation). Retrieved from http://ir.flo .org/nec/institutionalPublicationPublicView.action;jsessionid=61507D1 FB072E76A050C89B1AFEE62C8institutionalItemId=127

LeBorgne, W., & Rosenberg, M. (2014). *The vocal athlete.* San Diego, CA: Plural Publishing.

Miller, D. G. (2008). *Resonance in singing: Voice building through acoustic feedback.* Princeton, NJ: Inside View Press.

Monson, B. B., Hunter, E. J., Lotto, A. J., & Story, B. H. (2014). The perceptual significance of high-frequency energy in the human voice. *Frontiers in Psychology, 5,* 587.

Perta, K., Bae, Y., & Obert, K. (in press). A pilot investigation of twang quality using magnetic resonance imaging. *Logopedics Phoniatrics Vocology.*

Ragan, K., & Kapsner-Smith, M. (2019). Vehicular vocalizing to start your day. *Journal of Singing, 76*(2), 161–166.

Robbins, C. (2002). Why buzz? Putting Lessac's y-buzz to work. *Voice and Speech Trainers Association Newsletter, 16*(1), 6–8.

Sundberg, J. (1987). *The science of the singing voice.* Dekalb, IL: Northern Illinois University Press.

Sundberg, J. (1990). What's so special about singers? *Journal of Voice, 4*(2), 107–119.

Titze, I. (1994). *Principles of voice production.* Englewood Cliffs, NJ: Prentice Hall.

Titze, I., Bergan, C. C., Hunter, E. J., & Story, B. (2003). Source and filter adjustments affecting the perception of the vocal qualities twang and yawn. *Logopedics Phoniatrics Vocology, 28*(4), 147–155.

Titze, I. R. (2008). Nonlinear source-filter coupling in phonation: Theory. *Journal of the Acoustical Society of America, 123*(5), 2733–2749.

Titze, I., & Worley, A. (2009). Modeling source-filter interaction in belting and high-pitched operatic male singing. *The Journal of the Acoustical Society of America, 126*(3), 1530–1540.

Verdolini, K., Druker, D. G., Palmer, P. M., & Samawi, H. (1998). Laryngeal adduction in resonant voice. *Journal of Voice, 12*(3), 315–327.

Chapter 8

Sample Vocal Warm-Up Routines

Introduction

This chapter presents eight sample warm-ups. They are categorized by contemporary commercial music (CCM) or classical genres, by gender (see below), and a broadly suggested level of vocal development. Singers are encouraged to include the articulatory stretches and respiratory isolation exercises previously presented in the respective chapters as a part of a daily practice routine. Straw phonation, water bubbles, and kinesthetic singing tools outlined throughout the book are encouraged to be integrated within a warm-up regimen. For example, it is easy to include the barre3 ball, a large exercise ball, and the bands outlined in Chapter 3, the respiration chapter, in these warm-up protocols. Suggested vocal ranges (not the starting pitch) are located at the top-right corner of each musical notation, along with a reference to the number of the exercise if outlined within the book. Alternations to the vocal range are expected in order to accommodate singers' individual needs since, to keep the sample warm-ups broadly focused, specific voice types are not identified.

Chapter 1 includes a more extensive discussion on the difference between a vocal warm-up and vocal function exercises. A vocal warm-up can be accomplished in a few minutes or, depending on the circumstances, may require a more extended period of time. For example, if a classical singer is preparing to sing a principal role in a full-length opera that evening, they will spend less time warming up the voice so that the overall vocal dose is somewhat limited prior to the performance. If the same singer is warming up to sing two or three arias at an audition, they will want to be at the peak of the "bloom of the voice" (height of vocal efficiency) at the outset of the audition and may require a vocal warm-up for a longer duration. If a CCM singer is warming up the voice prior to a performance that requires a great deal of belt aesthetic, they will benefit from using head-dominant registration exercises in addition to chest-dominant exercises to properly prepare the instrument for the evening's performance. There is much to consider in order to arrive at a beneficial series of vocal tasks that serve each singer's individual needs.

The author acknowledges that there is gender diversity, so when exercises are referenced as being suitable for the male or female voice, nonbinary and/or transitioning singers may refer to whichever exercises are suitable to their vocal development. The use of the term avocational denotes someone who pursues singing, not as their primary mode of income. It must be acknowledged, however, that there is a broad range of singers within the avocational label from extremely serious to recreational. A series of vocal exercises intended to warm up the voice should be personalized to meet a singer's individual needs for vocal preparation.

Classical Female (Middle/High School, Undergraduate, Avocational Singer)

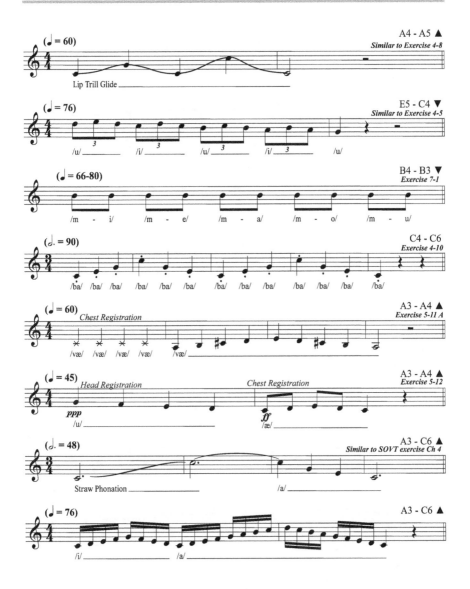

Classical Female (Undergraduate/Graduate, Emerging Professional, Professional Singer)

Classical Male (Middle/High School, Undergraduate, Avocational Singer)

Classical Male (Undergraduate/Graduate, Emerging Professional, Professional Singer)

CCM Female (Beginning/Intermediate)

CCM Female (Intermediate/Advanced)

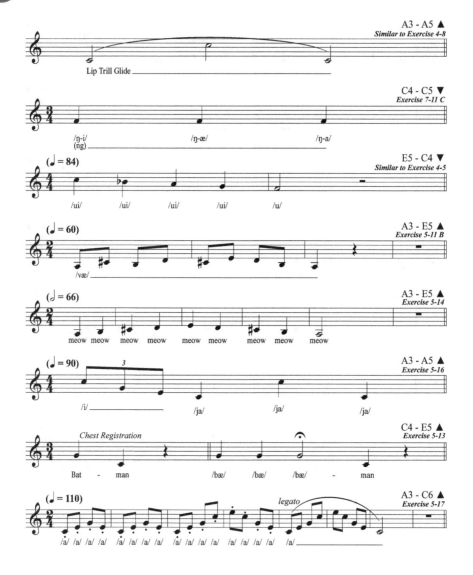

CCM Male (Beginning/Intermediate)

CCM Male (Intermediate/Advanced)

Index

Note: Page numbers in **bold** reference non-text material